BATTLE
OF THE
BOOKS
AND MORE

READING ACTIVITIES FOR
MIDDLE SCHOOL STUDENTS

Sybilla Cook, Frances Corcoran & Beverley Fonnesbeck

Alleyside Press®

Fort Atkinson, Wisconsin

Published by **Alleyside Press**, an imprint of Highsmith Press
Highsmith Press
W5527 Highway 106
P.O. Box 800
Fort Atkinson, Wisconsin 53538-0800
1-800-558-2110

The paper used in this publication meets the minimum requirements of American National Standard for Information Science — Permanence of Paper for Printed Library Material. ANSI/NISO Z39.48-1992.

Library of Congress Cataloging-in-Publication Data
    Cook, Sybilla Avery, 1930-
        Battle of the Books and more : reading activities for middle school
    students / Sybilla Cook, Frances Corcoran, and Beverley Fonnesbeck.
            p. cm.
        Includes bibliographical references.
        ISBN 1-57950-047-1 (alk. paper)
        1. Middle school libraries–Activity programs–United States. 2.
    Children's libraries–Activity programs–United States. 3. Book
    contests–United States. 4. Children–Books and reading–United States.
    5. Reading promotion–United States. 6. Children's literature–Study
    and teaching (Middle school)–United States. I. Corcoran, Frances. II.
    Fonnesbeck, Beverley, 1925- III. Title.
    Z675.S3 C75 2001
    028.5'5–dc21   2001000456
                                                    CIP

Contents

Acknowledgments

This book could not have been written without collaboration and cooperation from librarians and readers across the country. Book people of all stripes have always shared their enthusiasm through various informal and formal networks of newsletters, workshops, and library conferences. The Chicago Public Schools and cooperating radio stations held battles while Frances Corcoran was in elementary school. The idea caught fire once again in the 70's and has continued. We never know what influence our teaching has on the future. This is what makes "Battle of the Books" special, and has given it such a long life.

There are many special people who have contributed to this book. Robin M. Caton from Champaign-Urbana, Illinois was the original inspiration. Roz Goodman of Alaska has spent time encouraging us and proofreading the manuscript every step of the way. Cheryl Page co-authored the original book, *Books Battles and Bees* (ALA, 1994) to which this book is a successor. Marilyn Turchi of the Winnetka, Illinois schools gave initial help in starting the Battles in Des Plaines schools. Brenda Duff and the staff of the Ela Area District Library in Lake Zurich, Illinois helped update the book and added advice from the public library viewpoint. Readers Kate Campbell of Madison, Wisconsin and Rosalind Gjessing of Columbus, Ohio suggested some of their favorite books, as did librarians Cathi Rooth of Monmouth, Oregon, the staff of the Kahuku Public and School Library, Kahuku, Oahu, Hawaii, Katherine Gove and Katherine M. Gove of the G. A. R. Memorial Library in West Newbury, Massachusetts, Penny Clark of the Elkton (Oregon) Grade School, Carol Lamb and Dan White of the Douglas County Library System (Oregon). Lynda Russell of the Centennial Middle School and Jody Rutherford of Portland Public Schools in Oregon helped track down citations.

The web provided discussion and suggestion from those who are actively involved in reading programs throughout the United States. Some of these are Jamie Boston (Davis, California), Joan Enders (Kalama, Washington) Kathy Glockner (Winston, Oregon) Jonie Fitzsimmons (Fort Carson, Colorado), Tiki Levinson (Bristol Bay, Alaska), Frances Martindale (Providence, Rhode Island), Linda Paul (Wichita, Kansas), Linda Sears (Birmingham, Alabama), and Mary Ellen Tremblay (Petersburg, Alaska). Gretchen Baldauf of West Seneca, New York compiled a list of many suggestions on the LM_Net archival site, and some of these referred to the many books by Ellen Jay, another e-mail contributor. To all of these, and the many others we neglected to name, we owe a great debt.

Dedications

Sybilla Cook dedicates this book to grandchildren Alyssa, Ana, Averie, Matthew, and Thomas in the hopes they will continue to be enthusiastic readers.

Fran Corcoran's grandchildren Brandon, Tyler and Josh are beginning readers. Hopefully, they will have librarians and teachers who will find ways to make the job of learning to read exciting.

Beverley Fonnesbeck gives thanks to librarian friends for enjoying books with her over the years; to her daughter Alexandra for persuading the computer to behave; and to her new grandson, John Maxwell, for appearing just as she needed a new listener.

Introduction

Why should teachers and librarians use scarce time and resources to get involved with book contests like Battle of the Books? For one reason only—to inspire students to read. Competition is a great motivator.

Students offer these reasons for not reading:[1]

- it's boring

- I don't have the time

- it's too hard

- it's not important

- it's no fun.

Reading contests overcome all these objections. They're great incentives for leisure reading. They help students and teachers widen their knowledge of books beyond the most popular or well known.

The industrial society considered reading an important skill, though not necessary for everyone. In today's information society, it is *the* fundamental survival skill. Even leisure-time activities, such as computer programs and games, rely on the ability to read and respond appropriately.

The "State New Economy Index" ranks the states on their knowledge-based economy. Lucy Calkins refers to Jeff McQuillan's citation of an international study which found that "access to print" and "frequent silent reading time" were the most important correlations with reading achievement in several countries.[2] The 105th U.S. Congress funded the "Reading Excellence Act" in fiscal year 1998 to encourage family reading. This act defines reading as "the ability to read fluently" and "the development and maintenance of a motivation to read."[3]

A major goal for teacher/librarians is developing student interest in reading for pleasure—thus polishing and reinforcing skills learned in the classroom. We aim to create a love for reading that will translate itself into a lifelong reading habit. It's a challenge, since rival activities increasingly compete for student attention. According to current statistics, students spend one percent or less of their time in recreational reading.[4]

Benefits of Book Battles

Interaction with other students in friendly competition eliminates boredom. Students make time for what they enjoy, what their peers are doing is considered extremely important. One parent noted the Battle of the Books "set a fire under my children and got them to read." Parents want schools to help students get excited about learning, and contests are one way to turn students on to reading.

Administration, staff, and community members often become actively involved in these competitions. They are ideal subjects for newspaper or television features. An added benefit to this is that student reading and children's books become highly visible. One local newspaper writer enthused about "Battle of the Books," reporting "When I see kids excited about reading, it exhilarates me." This focus on the school library's relationship to the reading program creates excellent public relations.

Reading contests range anywhere from the simple spelling bee conducted in an individual classroom, to a formally structured program like "Battle of the Books." This book concentrates on the latter type of contest, because competition comes naturally to most middle school students.

Students enjoy demonstrating their knowledge of books. One high school valedictorian cited "Battle of the Books" in her graduation speech as one of the important experiences in her school years. Another student reported it was "one of the funnest things ever."

Performing before an audience, speaking clearly, and exhibiting good manners when another team is performing are skills we want students to demonstrate. Contests help develop these skills and performance goals. Since reading is primarily an isolated activity, being "on stage" is a new experience for many readers. For some, this may be their only formal competitive experience and their first opportunity to shine in front of peers and parents.

Current educational literature suggests school learning experiences should include academic, social, and individual growth. Book and reading contests often attract students who are not habitual readers. Students participating in reading contests meet others with similar interests but different reading abilities.

Cooperative learning and teamwork are often extolled as benefits from sports programs. Reading competitions bring these benefits to the non-athletic student. Cooperative learning occurs when teams "warm up" for the contests. Battle teams usually develop their own methods of dividing the responsibility for reading the titles on the list. Teams work toward a deadline, practice together, and expect each member to carry his or her own weight. A speaker or leader is selected to offer the group's answer in the actual battle.

Today's competitive world needs gracious winners, and losers who accept loss and survive to challenge another day. Individual competition has a way of either inflating or humbling the ego, but team competition provides support for losers as well as winners.

About This Book

Though our focus is on the middle school student, we attempt to give enough background so that you can design a reading contest fitting your students' particular needs.

The book includes all the "nitty gritty"—things learned from others, and those learned the hard way through personal experience. You'll find out how to save time through advance planning, and learn tips on reaching out to the school board, district administrators, and the wider community.

The book covers different types of programs, how to select appropriate titles, and how to write questions. To make it user friendly and save time, five sample questions are included for each of the books on our list. The questions are on a selection of books frequently read in the middle school years.

We've also included suggestions for using the Internet to enhance student learning and build relationships with the outside world. You can use these websites as sources for yourself or as inspiration to students.

We hope this book will make it easy for you to implement a reading contest in your school or library, and hope that you enjoy the experience as much as we have.

Endnotes

1. "Students Who Can Read, but Don't…" Reading is Fundamental, 1992.

2. Calkins, Lucy, Kate Montgomery, and Donna Santman, with Beverly Falk Heinemann. *A Teacher's Guide to Standardized Reading Tests: Knowledge is Power.* Greenwood Press, 1998. p. 47.

3. International Reading Association. "Summary of Title VIII-Reading Excellence Act, Educations Appropriations of 1999: a Bill to Amend the Elementary and Secondary Education Act of 1965 to Provide for Reading Excellence,"1998. URL: www.reading.org/advocacy/specialrep/REAsum01.htm. December 27, 2000.

4. Carnegie Council on Adolescent Development. *A Matter of Time: Risk and Opportunity in the Non-School Hours.* Carnegie Corporation of New York, 1992.

Cooperation and Preparation

You are convinced! A contest is precisely the thing to strengthen connections between the school library and the classroom, energize your students, encourage reading, and create an exciting and enjoyable learning experience for all. It's also a great way to promote wonderful titles that spend too much time on the shelves.

Choosing the Format

Quiz contests are often used as reinforcement for learning. They can be used encourage students to work together in teams and learn problem solving skills by working with other team members. The contests can take many forms, depending on the goals of the district, school, and/or library.

Where do you go from here? Whether you are a school or a public librarian, there are many things to consider. What books will you use? How many books, and how will they be chosen? What reading levels will be represented? How many questions will you need, and who will write them?

Will you begin with a single class, a grade level, or an entire school? If you choose one or two classes, which ones will they be? How will students be chosen?

If your program is school-wide or city-wide, how structured will it be? How will contests be conducted? What will be the rules? How, and by whom, will decisions be made? Where and how will contests take place? Will each event be an end in itself, or will a tournament structure evolve? Whom can you call on for help?

Battle of the Books

Battle of the Books is more complex than other contests. While battles can be conducted within a single classroom, they provide more enjoyment and incentive when they take place among several classrooms or between schools. For example, Alaska uses a tournament form. Participating schools select winners who then battle within their districts. The district winners finally meet in a statewide battle. The school library provides an ideal venue for these larger undertakings, since the librarian is in touch with all of the classes, knows the students and the books, and can coordinate the program with the various teachers.

Teams usually consist of two to five students, depending on the class size within a given school or district. There are various ways of forming these teams. Some schools have teams that compete for fun; others have teams where winning is the main motivation. Sometimes teachers recommend students for a team. Some schools have preliminary tests, and those who score highest make the teams. Middle school students usually prefer to choose their own teams. In one school, students write down their name and three students with whom they would like to be teamed. The librarian then puts together the teams, attempting to balance those who work well together, those who need to be separated, and those with varied general skill levels. You can also tap students who haven't chosen to participate by telling them that someone picked them to be on their team.[2]

It's wise to avoid changes to the team roster once players are selected. Middle school friendships are volatile, and constant change can bring chaos to long-term battle plans.

You also need to decide on a substitute policy. Students miss school for a variety of reasons, and a one- or two-person team is at a real disadvantage against a full slate. In one school, some teams pressured weaker members to miss school on a battle day so a stronger reader could be substituted! We learned to maintain our own list of alternates from which to select the substitute.

Teams enjoy choosing names, creating buttons or T-shirts, and seeking other ways to identify themselves. These activities can help to maintain interest in the contest while books are being read.

Who Will Take Part?

After investigating various formats for book contests, you must next decide how the participants will be selected. Some people believe book promotions, like other "enrichment activities," should be targeted to gifted students or advanced readers—those who need to do more than regular classroom activities. However, experience shows that all students benefit from contest excitement and gain satisfaction by sharing reading experiences with the entire group.

Often less-motivated students gain far more than those who read often and regularly. They make a greater effort for the sake of the team, with their stronger partners providing support and encouragement. There is serendipity for the audience as well—we've noticed that interest in the titles battled usually shows up in later check-out statistics.

Cooperative learning is inherent in the interaction of battle teams. While a few groups will operate in a relatively laissez-faire atmosphere, many assign specific books to each member. Some quiz each other regularly, and spend their free time discussing books on the list.

Choosing the Books

While contests benefit students in many ways, the book experience is what each event is really about. Choice of books is vital to the success of any reading activity. Variety is necessary to meet different tastes, and to encourage appreciation of different genres. Include books that generate excitement and enthusiasm about characters that live, stories that validate life, words that flow, and values that endure. No matter which contest format is chosen, students will become deeply involved with the books on the list. Selections must be the best that they can be.

Multiple copies of each title should be available, and you need to allow enough time for all participants to read the books. It's wonderful when a teacher chooses a title as a read-aloud, but it also means the book will be checked out to a single class-room for at least two weeks.

Hundreds of titles match these criteria. How is the choice made? In the end, librarians call upon their professional skills to provide suitable choices for the students and teachers they serve. Numerous resources are available to assist in the task, but each school and set of students are unique. Each librarian and/or teacher will know how to select those books that best suit the students in their school from our suggested lists.

Selection resources include lists of books commended by state library associations, state departments of education, and school districts. The American Library Association and other organizations serving students and youth offer extensive and sometimes extensively annotated book lists. Many of these are now available on the Internet. Other websites contain book selection guidance and support. If there is a problem with choice, it is in having too many titles from which to choose. Many websites are listed in Chapter 5, "Working with the Web."

Begin with your own library collection. Survey your shelves and note over-looked titles that should not be forgotten. If you have an annual state contest for a favorite title, include some of the nominees in your list. You'll promote that program as well.

An important factor in selecting titles for competition is the level of complexity the story provides. Each book must be able to support a number of questions without descending to trivia. Many apparently simple stories, such as *Frindle* by Andrew Clements, have been successfully used because of their strong plot and theme. Most series books, including Harry Potter, and/or hi-lo vocabulary titles have inter-changeable plots and paper characters that don't meet this criterion.

How many books do you need on a list? The answer depends, of course, upon the number of participants, the size of your library collection, and the length and complexity of your program. Some schools have used as few as 10 titles, while others include as many as 100. Alaska's official list contains 15 books for each of the five grade levels: K–2, 3–4, 5–6, 7–8, and high school.[1]

Heavy participation in Alaska's programs requires multiple copies of each title in each participating school. Titles available in paperback are selected whenever possible. Funds for purchasing copies come through donations from groups, PTA fundraisers, bake sales, and book sales. Preferential pricing by local book stores often includes substantial discounts.

An Illinois school district selected 40 titles for their district-wide program.[3] School-level battles were held once a month on 10 of the titles. Some of these schools shared the books with their sister schools, and would exchange their titles and questions in alternate months. At year's end the winning teams from each participating public and private school joined in a final battle at the public library.

Students who participate every year will need new challenges to keep them interested. If you are using a short list of books, change all titles each year. If your list is long, change about a third of the titles annually. Alaska's list, for example, changes every year, but 25 percent of the titles are reused after a year has passed. Another Illinois district rotates titles for grades 3, 4, and 5 on a three-year cycle.

Cooperation and Planning

The important keys to success are cooperation and planning, whether your contests include several classes or are limited to one or two. As soon as you have an idea about the format, share it with other staff. Principals usually want to be consulted. If teachers are involved in helping to create the program, they are more likely to become avid supporters. Early consultation with others will spur your own enthusiasm, bring new ideas into play, and ensure a strong and continuing support as the process unfolds.

The staff will often suggest book titles and may have also ideas on selecting students and scheduling. Library volunteers and parents of participating students can serve as questioners or judges. Youth service librarians in public libraries will appreciate the link between their libraries and the school. A meeting of representatives from any or all of these groups can be an enjoyable and stimulating event.

If you cannot meet with all participants at once, be sure to contact each one separately, and provide a rationale and requests for input to all concerned. After the team registration closes, one public library has a mandatory meeting for the team members and their parents to review the rules. Everyone receives a written copy to make sure they know what is expected.

Student enthusiasm is quickly ignited, but the flame must be fanned. Plan a special introduction for your classes. You might have a short book bee, or even a relay race. Point out how much fun competing in a friendly way can be, and how cooperation with teammates adds to the fun of outscoring other teams. Explain the plans for the book contest in which they will both compete and cooperate. Be ready, of course, to hear student suggestions, which often prove useful.

Introduce the books and have them available for students to review. If you and your advisory committee have selected more books than you plan to use, allow students to vote for the final choices.

Publish your final plans and book list in the school bulletin, parent newsletter, and local newspapers if appropriate. Make presentations to the school board and parent groups. Involve students. Provide handouts and flyers to other libraries in your area. Ask local book stores to post the list and have copies of the books for sale. Make posters for them if they are willing to use them. Some schools and districts have websites that can bring your plans and graphics to an ever-growing audience.

Let everyone know that a reading event is about to happen. Have students design posters to display around the school and local libraries, as well as the post office and other public places. Then, let the contest begin!

Endnotes

1. "Battle of the Books Handbook," 1985. (Alaska Association of School Librarians, Anchorage, photocopy.)

2. Mary Ellen Tremblay. "Hit: Battle of Books team selection." Posted on the ERIC Archives of LM_NET messages, December 13, 1999, 13:47:48. URL: http://www.askeric.org

3. "Presenting Battle of the Books," (District #62, Des Plaines, Illinois, 1980, photocopy.)

Contests and Adaptations

Contests have always been popular with students and adults. Book quizzes based on knowledge of books range from an impromptu game based on 20 questions—"I'm thinking of a book." "Is it about an animal?"—to the formal structure of Battle of the Books. They can take place anywhere, from a lunch table to a stage set.

Classroom teachers often develop motivational games based on baseball, basketball, or football. Students who answer questions correctly advance paper footballs on a chalkboard field, shoot sponge basketballs into a net, or move around the room from chairs representing bases.

Popular game shows like *Who Wants to Be a Millionaire?*, *Jeopardy*, *What's My Line?*, *Wheel of Fortune* and *Hollywood Squares* also lend themselves to curriculum adaptations. *The Ultimate Guide to Student Contests: Grades 7–12*[1] lists several categories of national contests for students sponsored by non-profit and commercial groups. Some are adaptable to your own programs, and you can use others to complement activities in your school or library.

Battle of the Books

Though Battle of the Books is structured, it is easily adapted to the needs of individual classes within a school. A search of the archives at LM_NET[2] a worldwide discussion group for school library media specialists and people involved in the school library media field, turned up many postings about Battle of the Books. These show a number of variations in the numbers of titles used, how students are chosen for teams, how questions are phrased, and other related activities.

Wichita, Kansas, for example, does competitive book talks in conjunction with their program. The names of titles on their book list are put in a hat, and each team draws three. They choose one to use in their three-minute presentation about the book before a panel composed of two judges.

Choice of Books

Sometimes a Battle of the Books committee is in charge of the choice of books, but generally the titles are chosen by individual school library media specialists and teachers. They are usually drawn from different genres. The lists range from 10 to 100 titles. In some schools, different books are assigned to different grade levels.

Teams

Schools may work with teams of three, four, or five students. They may choose a captain or spokesperson who states the answer to the team's questions. Teams may have a designated substitute, but most schools don't allow other students to fill in for absent members—teams battle with only the members who are present.

Teams may come from the entire school population, or may represent just one classroom. They often go on to battle other district schools in their districts. Alaska's schools, which are spread out across a large state, battle stateside, using audio-conferencing equipment. This coming year, they plan to pilot "Chat Room Battles."

Four independent schools in Rhode Island have set up battles among themselves. The teams are formed from students from all participating schools—Gordon, Wheeler, and Lincoln in Providence and St. Michael's School in Newport. Wheeler and Lincoln School have exchanged student-written questions. One group of fourth graders battles another fourth grade by e-mail.

Questions and Answers

In almost all cases, 20 questions are used in each battle. Each team has a 30-second time period to answer the question posed to them. If they don't answer correctly, the question goes to the opposing team. Teams are allowed to confer during the 30 seconds. In some schools, any member of the team can call out answers. In others, only one answer can be given—usually by the team captain or spokesperson.

Alaska has successfully tried a new format.[3] Each team gets the same question and has 30 seconds to answer. They write the title and author's last name on paper or on a white erase board. When the time is up, they show their answers to the questioner. Points are awarded to the teams that respond correctly. This eliminates the possibility of one team getting easy questions while the other gets the hard ones. If there is a "bad" question, both teams get it. If no one answers correctly, the battle continues with no additional points scored.

The answer is usually the title of the book. Some schools require the author be given, while others give extra points for correctly naming the author. Some require only the last name of the author be given, while others expect both first and last names be stated.

Alaska gives points for successful challenges to questions. If a team responds with an answer that doesn't match the official one, the questioner asks if the team would like to challenge. The team is then given a copy of the book and three minutes to find a reference to their response in the book and then state their challenge with the page reference(s)—sometimes implied information may cover more than one page or chapter. The judge then decides if the challenge is valid. (It helps if the questioner or judge has read the books.) Sometimes the answer isn't given in the exact words on a given page, but it will show up over a number of pages or chapters.

As one Alaska school librarian says, "The neat thing about challenges is that it addresses the issue of higher level thinking skills. Kids really have to know the books, think the questions through, find the supporting evidence, and state their case. On rare occasions, teams may get carried away by the opportunity to challenge, but it's easy to end that by saying if a team does not succeed at challenging three times, they can't challenge again. It's rare that the challenge opportunity gets abused." [4]

Audience Participation

It's exciting when other students and parents come to watch a battle. It's easier to keep the audience's attention by including them in the activity. Often, students from other classes who are watching the battles are given chances to answer if both teams fail to answer correctly. A school in Kalama (Washington) hands out a sign with their teacher's name to each watching class. When the question goes to the audience, the class that raises their sign first gets the chance to answer and earn points for their class. Four Rhode Island schools write cheers celebrating reading and/or the battle. They chant these before the first round, and between each of the following rounds.

Rewards

Certificates are often given to students who take part in Battle of the Books. However, the most valued rewards are when students see their names on a bulletin board or in a school newsletter. It's even better if they find their name in the local newspaper—something that happens rarely for the non-athlete.

Some schools reward team members with pins or t-shirts with the team name or logo. Some participants' names are drawn for small prizes like books or pizza coupons. The names of winning teams can be added to a perpetual plaque or trophy for the school display case. One local bookstore in Alaska gives a $5.00 gift certificate to all district winners.

Public Participation

Many schools assign a coach to each team. These may be teachers, interested parents, or other volunteers. The coaches help teams learn cooperation skills, practice analyzing questions and strategies for answering, and write their own questions for practice rounds. Parents also make good scorekeepers and timekeepers. The more members of the community that come into the schools to see and take part in positive programs, the better. And the school libraries get some welcome visibility.

A school in Fort Carson (Colorado) prepares "information logs"—forms students can use when taking notes on the books they have read. Their librarian says it usually takes one battle for the kids to see the value of the forms. After that, they become converted. They use the notes to study before battles and to share with absent team members. The forms are also helpful to team parents who read some of the books to their students at night.

Playoffs take place within a school, or a school district, or at the public library. Parents, administrators, and other community members can be invited to these. The Wichita (Kansas) District brings in local television anchors to moderate district battles, thus ensuring a larger audience.

Higher Level Thinking

Most schools use questions that are answered by the title of the book. These are simple recall questions, ordinarily not open to interpretation. For example: "Which book is about a boy named Tom who likes to swindle people?" (The answer is *The Great Brain*, by John D. Fitzgerald.)

Some librarians or teachers prefer questions based on more advanced levels of thinking and understanding. The article on "Greater Dimensions for the Battle of the Books" in the *School Librarian's Workshop*[5] addresses this topic, referring to Bloom's six cognitive levels of Knowledge, Comprehension, Application, Synthesis, Analysis, and Evaluation.

You can use comparison and analysis questions in a battle. Questions can be created about a common theme, such as survival, a historical period, or particular characters.

An occasional contest could be created to stress these higher-level skills. If there is a lengthy booklist, you can ask a question like "In which two books does a school serve as the setting?" or "In which two books do animals talk like people?" Comparison skills are called for if you, "Name at least one way in which *The True Adventures of Charlotte Doyle*[6] is like *The Slave Dancer*."[7] Possible answers might refer to the sailing ship setting, the fact that both books take place in the 1800s, or that both books have captains at odds with their crews. A correct answer would be worth five points, and knowledge of the author would be two points. You could allow the other team to add another item, or to challenge an answer they feel is wrong.

Thinking skills can also be developed through the use of "why" questions. Ruth Harshaw's original book *What Book Is That?* contains questions of this type.[8] "Why" questions can focus attention on the idea of consequences, specific actions causing specific events. For example, "Why were Dicey and her brothers and sisters walking to Aunt Cilla's instead of going by bus?"[9] or "Why was a tennis star spending his summer on a berry farm?"[10] One book that lends itself really well to this type of approach is Avi's 1991 Newbery Honor Book, *Nothing But the Truth* (Orchard 1991), which shows how a minor action can escalate into a crisis.

If you use this sort of question, give five points for the answer, with three points for the title and two points for the author. You also need to allow more time for the contest, since the questions will take longer to answer. Questioners and judges need to be well-versed about the books' plots, themes, and characters. Classroom teachers can follow up by having students develop possible alternate outcomes.

Other Reading Activities

Another method which encourages higher level thinking is to involve students in reading discussion groups such as Junior Great Books.[11] These are based on a process called "reflective thinking," which "requires a suspension of judgment, a conscious effort to hold back evaluation until evidence is collected and interpreted."[12] Students learn to use a book's specific concepts as a basis for discussion, rather than relying on their own knowledge or ideas. They learn to group and categorize books in terms of concept and theme.

This method can also be adapted to themes and concepts. Choose several books on a given theme or time period, such as World War II, and ask students to form a hypothesis about life in that time. After they read the books, have a discussion in which they prove or disprove their hypothesis.

Many teachers and librarians make up supplementary activity project cards for students. Some of these also incorporate other types of thinking skills. The *Alaska Battle of the Books Handbook*[13] suggests such activities as using computer programs to create crossword puzzles about individual books. Students can learn a great deal about books by designing board games, card games such as *Concentration*, or adaptations of television quiz shows.

Those interested in technology can create electronic book displays using programs such as KidPix, Hyperstudio, and Digital Chisel or Powerpoint.

Over to You

Think about which of these variations will work in your school. As you talk to teachers abut the program, ask for their ideas and opinions. The more input they have in the process, the more enthusiastic they will be. If you aren't sure how to implement these suggestions, or are looking for other ideas, try a listserv such as LM_NET. This provides library professionals with a forum to share ideas and information, and make contacts with others. You undoubtedly will find someone who can answer your questions on why and how they do things the way they do. After all, librarians like sharing information!

Endnotes

1. Pendleton, Scott. *The Ultimate Guide to Student Contests; Grades 7—2.* Walker & Co, 1977.

2. http://ericir.syr.edu/lm_net/

3. "Battle of the Books Handbook," 1985. (Alaska Association of School Librarians, Anchorage, photocopy.)

4. Goodman Dillingham, Roz. Alaska School District, e-mail communication with author, November 5, 1999.

5. "Greater Dimensions for the Battle of the Books" in the *School Librarian's Workshop*, September 1988, pp. 1–3.

6. Avi, *The True Confessions of Charlotte Doyle.* Orchard Books, 1990.

7. Fox, Paula. *The Slave Dancer.* Bradbury, 1973.

8. Harshaw, Ruth. *What Book is That?* Macmillan, 1948.

9. Voigt, Cynthia. *Dicey's Song.* Fawcett, 1995.

10. Olson, Gretchen. *Joyride.* Boyds Mills Press, 1998.

11. Great Books Foundation. *A Manual for Co-leaders.* The Foundation, 1965. (For information, write or call The Great Books Foundation, Suite 2300, Chicago, Illinois 60601-2298. Phone: 800-222-5870.)

12. Ibid.

13. "Battle of the Books Handbook," 1985.

Beyond Book Reports Reading Enhancements

Fun should always be part of the library program—after all, this is where lifelong attitudes toward reading begin. Though reading is often a solitary activity, sharing books can turn it into a social event.

It's both fun and a challenge to try different methods of weaving favorite books into the school curriculum. Since students learn in a variety of different ways, they benefit from a variety of activities. These activities also reach teachers. A dedicated bulletin board in the teachers' lounge can inform the staff about ideas and tips you learn from web surfing, useful magazine articles, new books, and what's going on in the library. Another way to promote books is to post lists of new books inside or outside the school rest rooms.

Book Discussion Groups

Book discussions not only promote books, but require students to demonstrate their understanding of what they read. One high school asked every faculty member to choose a favorite book from the collection, read it during the summer, and then lead a discussion group at the library. Students could sign up for the group they wanted to join. Some chose a group to find out about a particular book; others chose a group because they liked the teacher.

In 1983, Dell Publishing Company distributed a useful little pamphlet on book discussion groups.[1] Teachers serve as book talk coordinators. Thirty or so books are selected, an annotated book list is prepared, and a class session is spent discussing the books on the list. Students then sign up for the book talks they wish to attend.

The Junior Great Books discussion format is a highly structured format using many advanced thinking skills. The focus is on what the author intended to communicate to the reader. A speaker's assumptions can be challenged by others, and must be proved by a citation in the book.

Similar strategies can be used when students are reading the same book, or when all are reading books on a given theme. These can range from unstructured random conversations on the book, to formal discussions. Battle of the Books has a formal structure, but the way in which students acquire the necessary knowledge varies from school to school.

The activities that follow have been gathered from many sources—conferences, classes, networking with teachers and librarians, books, the Internet, and our personal experiences. For convenience, they are divided into three categories: those best for small groups, ones that work well in the classroom, and those, like

Battle of the Books, that reach beyond the classroom into the school district and community.

Individual and Small Group Activities

- **Reading Journals.** Have students keep "reading journals." This activity can be expanded by having the students bind their own journals. One librarian has students fill out simple forms, which she retains until the student moves to the middle school. She says students love to see their reading history.

- **Stuffed Animals.** Encourage students to dress up a stuffed animal like a book character. Some students might even be creative enough to adapt names like the ones in the VanderBear series of toy bears.

- **Book Reviews.** Have students write these, then post them for others to read. Suggest they try selling their book to others.

- **Presents.** Encourage students to choose a book they think a friend would like. Suggest they wrap it up, and give it to a friend with a note explaining why they chose it.

- **Print vs. Audiovisual.** Have students read a book, then watch a video version, and compare similarities and differences.

- **Trading Cards.** Have students make a set of trading cards for the characters in a book.

- **Board Games.** Assist students in making games representing plot points in a book. (Books of journey, such as *The Golden Compass*,[2] are ideal. Chutes and Ladders and Parcheesi are good models for books with an in-depth plot. Old Maid is a good one to use for book with many characters. Another good game model is Pictionary, where students illustrate particular titles.

- **Card Games.** Assist students in making cards illustrating characters in different well-known fairy tales or legends. These can be used for such games as Snap or Concentration.

- **Puzzle Creation.** Have students make up riddles or puzzles, such as crosswords and word searches.

- **Biography Bags.** Have students fill a paper bag with items relating to the subject of a biography. A book on Eisenhower might have a map of Europe, toy army men, a picture of the Presidential Seal, and so forth. Peanuts would be a natural for a bag on George Washington Carver, along with samples of products made from these.

  Display all finished biography bags in the library. If the subjects' names are taken off, the bags can be used as a mix and match game for other students. These try to find out who is represented by the articles in the various bags.

- **Paper Dolls.** Encourage students to create paper dolls from book characters, and design wardrobes suitable for different events in the book. (The Ramona paper doll book is a great model for this activity.)

- **Map Making.** Work with students in making a map showing the settings of a book and the character's journey. Perhaps the social studies teacher can get involved.

- **Puppets.** Have students make shadow puppets to create a play or recreate a scene in the story.

- **Electronic Book Reports.** These can be created using Kidpix, Hyperstudio, Digital Chisel, Powerpoint.

Classroom and Middle Size Group Activities

- **Interactive Bulletin Boards.** Design ones relating to the World Series, the Olympics, the Indianapolis 500, the Iditarod, or any other student interest. After students read a book, they can move their baseball, or sled, or whatever, around the course.

- **I'm Thinking Of… Game.** The instructor begins with that phrase, and continues to describe a book until someone comes up with the answer. That student, in turn says "I'm thinking of…" and describes a book of his or her choice.

- **Read Aloud.** Choose a read-aloud book to be read over a period of days at a dedicated time, and announce what will be read on a poster outside the library. Classroom teachers can give tickets to interested students. After listening the tickets are put in a box. One of these is drawn every two weeks for a paperback book.

- **Reader's Theater.** Students participate by choosing parts and reading each character's dialogue aloud. Select a chapter or tantalizing part of the story to draw the listener into the plot and thus the book.

- **Hidden books.** Hide a book in a canvas bag, and hang it next to a large piece of poster board. Students can write questions on the poster board about the book. Questions must be capable of being answered with a "yes" or "no." The librarian or teacher writes in the answer when it is convenient. Students continue to ask questions until they have the correct title.

- **Genres.** Put up a sheet of poster paper for each genre. Ask students to first write descriptions of the genres. Later they can add sample titles.

- **Readings and Endings.** Read from the book's beginning, and ask students to write an ending for the book based on the first chapter happenings.

- **Charades.** Have students act out the title of a book.

- **Comparisons.** Each student reads a different book on a particular topic, such as pioneers. Ask them to compare similarities and differences between the pioneer life as portrayed in the book, and their own life today. Create a chart of these differences—such as how many clothes people own—and ask small groups of students to work cooperatively to fill it in.

- **Treasure Hunt.** Write literary clues about a book, and hide them in the library or classroom. Make up a trivia game about a book.

- **Scavenger Hunt.** Send students on a hunt through the library for particular kinds of books. It may be one with a certain number of pages, a particular illustrator or publisher, about a particular person, place or animal, a particular title, and so on. In Florida, a librarian assembles items that have a tie-in to a book, and students have to match the item to the book. (Keep in mind the possibility of re-shelving problems.)

- **Run of Cards.** Write literary clues on the back of playing cards, and give the cards out as "prizes" when teaching library skills. When they are all handed out, the students find others with matching suits (hearts, clubs, etc.) and then put their clues together to guess the title of a book.

- **Book Baseball.**

  - Divide the class into two teams.

  - Arrange 3 "bases" plus "home plate" around the room.

  - Use baseball rules to determine "runs" and "outs" etc.

  - The leader or "pitcher" reads a question about a book that can be answered by either title or author. Either a correct title or author answer lets the student advance one base.

  - If both title and author are correctly given, the student advances two bases. If incorrect, the student is "out," sits down, and the next "batter" goes up to bat.

  - After three outs, the other team has a chance to bat, or the teacher decides time is up. You can also set a timer.

- **Wheel of Reading.** (This is based on a combination of Hangman and Wheel of Fortune.) You need something to write on—chalkboard, easel, etc.—that is large enough for everyone to see.

  - Choose a category: author, title, incident, character…

  - On the board put one underline mark for each letter of the answer.

  - One student at a time guesses the letters. They keep going until they miss. If they miss, they get the head of a hangman.

  - The next student gets a turn, and so on.

  - Keep playing until the correct answer is given. Then, put another set of underlines on the board.

- **Puzzle Clues.** (from Ela Library in Lake Zurich, Illinois)

  - Choose a picture to represent each letter of the alphabet.

  - Hide the pictures around the room.

  - Each week, present a sentence (in picture format—no letters) to be decoded.

  - Clues may be given to the solution of the puzzle: (i.e. this book gives you the mileage from Honolulu to Chicago.)

  - Students first decode the alphabet, then use their own code sheet for decoding subsequent puzzles. Even problem readers can do this.

- Provide a mailbox for the decoded messages. At the end of the week, reward all the winners, or have a drawing from all the winners for a few prizes.

Correlation With Art and Music Programs

- **Stickers.** Students can make their own stickers for books. Students draw a character, incident, etc. in black ink on white paper. Reduce the picture on the photocopier to the size of an address label. Then run off the pictures on sheets of address labels, available in various sizes and colors from office supply stores. You can usually fit pictures from several students on one sheet.

- **Postcards.** Have the students create postcards about the books they have read. The front of the postcard should illustrate the book. The author's name and the book title can be placed on the back. These can be printed out using the appropriate software—word processing and/or drawing or printshop program, and students can sell sets of these postcards as a fundraising activity.

- **Decorations.** Students can draw scenes on fabric squares with colored markers or fabric crayons. These can later be pieced together for a wall hanging, bulletin board backing, or draperies in the library or school office.

- **Art Lessons.** Use picture books as a framework for art lessons. Students can find examples of collage, charcoal, watercolor, etc. in picture books.

- **T-Shirts.** Design an illustration for a book, and make T-shirts using the design. Use crayons, or special computer transfers.

- **Puppets.** Make stick, shadow or paper bag puppets of book characters, and use them to tell about a book.

- **Masks.** Design masks for the book characters. These can be used in connection with a readers theater presentation.

- **Murals.** Assist the students in making a large mural about a book or books. Cut holes where the character's faces would be. Students can put their own heads through as they talk about a book.

- **Jigsaw Puzzles.** Have students draw a large picture of a scene from a book. Glue or laminate it on cardboard, and then cut it up into puzzle pieces. Other students can enjoy putting the puzzle back together. (Note: It's a good idea to have students put their initials on the back of their own puzzle pieces. This will keep the pieces from being mixed up with other puzzle illustrations.)

- **Songs.** Ask students to make up a song about a book using a well-known tune, such as "The Bear Went Over the Mountain" or "99 Bottles of Pop on the Wall." Each verse can be based on a different scene from the book. Use some of the books and songs for music classes.

Correlation with Gifted and Talented Programs

- **Webbing.** Have students pick a topic or theme such as animal life, families, or survival. First, they should write down all the ideas they can think of that pertain to the subject: how animals live, different kinds of families; what one needs to survive on one's own. These ideas form the nodes on the web. From these nodes, students can branch out into books on the reading list—and others—that provide different kinds of useful information about the topic in question. From the answers found in these books, students could go on and research other types of information in encyclopedias, non-fiction books, magazines, the World Wide Web, videos, CDs, etc. For webbing, you can use a program like Inspiration. (Engaging Minds, LLC, Tel: (541) 330-6284, Email: enminds@az.com) or the site *Graphic Organizer* at www.graphic.org.

- **Calendar.** Have students design a literary riddle calendar to be used in the library. Use a calendar with the largest daily squares you can find. Use self-sticking notes or cut blank pieces of paper the same size as the calendar squares. Use these squares to write clues about a particular book. You will need four separate clues. Post one on Monday, another on Tuesday, and so on. Provide an answer box for other students. If someone solves it on Monday, they get four points; Tuesday's solvers earn three points, and so on. On Friday, post the title of the book along with all those who answered correctly. On the following Monday, begin clues to another book. At the end of a month, students with the most earned points receive a prize.

- **Board Games.** Have students design a large Monopoly-type board game that younger students can play. Instead of money, they collect "book pages," and the one with the most pages at the end of the game wins. The board should have squares with illustrations from familiar books, lucky squares where they can draw cards with questions about books (tell the name of a book about a bear who likes honey and get "x" number of pages), and lots of squares where they jump ahead or fall back.

- **Fact and Opinion.** "Gifted" students think they know a great deal, because they remember well, but often they have not learned to cross-check their opinions. Comparing fiction and nonfiction books with encyclopedias and information on websites is a useful project for these students. Biographies, historical fiction, science books, and realistic fiction books all lend themselves to this type of research project.

School-wide Activities

- **Book Award Program.** If your state sponsors a book award program where titles are chosen by students, encourage your students to get involved. Purchase three to 10 paperback copies of each title, promote the books, circulate them to interested teachers for read alouds, do booktalks, and have a big election. Some states have websites for their book award programs.

- **Sleepover Read-a-thons.** Plan a special night where students can sleep over in the library. Prepare book-related activities and food. The LM_NET listserv archives has a compilation of suggestions for these events.[3]

- **Audiovisual Productions.** Many schools put on daily or weekly TV or radio shows. Different classes could provide weekly segments on favorite books, using any of the activities described above.

- **Reading Marathons.** Any combination of students, school staff, parents, and administrators can form a group to read in a marathon. Participants take turns reading aloud from a particular book for five minute "legs" before passing the book on to another member. The marathon can last for a given period of time, or continue until an entire book is read.

- **Video Teasers.** Have student volunteers create a panel discussion or short skit to introduce a book, telling just enough to make others interested in reading the book. Video tape these teasers, and use them for book award promotions, for the Newbery and Caldecott winners, book battles, or other special programs.

- **Decorated Doors.** Students decorate their classroom doors to represent favorite books. If the title is left off, it can also be a contest for other classes to guess the title of the book the door represents.

- **Parade Floats.** Students make floats on wagons to represent a favorite book or character. These can be paraded through elementary schools or through the neighborhood for Children's Book Week or National Library Week.

Endnotes

1. Fusco, Esther. *Everybody Reads: A Step-By-Step Guide to Establishing a Book Discussion Group in Your School.* Dell, 1983.

2. Pullman, Philip. *The Golden Compass.* Del Rey, 1999.

3. LM_NET@listserv.syr.edu

Networking with the Web

Prepare to add the thrill of cyberspace to the excitement of reading! Few innovations have had greater impact on the teaching-learning process so immediately or extensively as computer access to the Internet. While librarians and teachers learn to use the power of this new way to method of accessing information, they are also challenged to find the best means of using the technology to promote enthusiasm for books and reading. Reading computer screens can be tedious and difficult, but the opportunity to interact with authors and discuss books with others outside the local school can motivate students to read and learn.

The Internet has much to offer planners of reading activities and book contests. In addition to interacting with other librarians, the Web can be used to increase students' knowledge of books and authors. University schools of education provide extensive material for both teachers and students to enliven the world of reading. Some examples are the University of Albany's tutorials on using websites at *www.albany.edu/library/internet/checklist.html,* and the Columbia Education Center's Curriculum Exchange where teachers can find a variety of lesson plans at *http://ofcn.org/cyber.serv/academy/ace/lang/inter.html.* Most major publishers have websites that give students opportunities to respond to literature and interact with authors of favorite books.

Key questions need to be answered before integrating reading activities into the electronic arena:

1. Are appropriate and sufficient hardware and software available? What support is available?

2. What type of classroom or library configuration will give the best opportunity for students to share available computers?

3. What safeguards are needed to maintain the integrity of the search process and keep students on task?

While computers and Internet connections have become widespread in more affluent school districts, many elementary and middle schools may still lack the necessary hardware, software, and communication networks to put large numbers of students at the keyboards. As you consider using the Internet in your reading programs, begin by determining how many machines are available and under what conditions.

Once connected to the Internet, you can set up a buddy system for members of the battle teams. A buddy system is a plan for pairing friends on home computers, so they can work together. Survey parents to acquaint them with the importance of having computer technology in the school, and to learn how many students have a computer available at home. You can send lists of Internet sites that relate to reading to parents. Book lists can be placed on the school or library web page. Contest results can be posted. This interaction with parents may lead to their becoming library advocates.

Remember the World Wide Web is not selective. In their excellent manual, *Teaching with the Internet*,[1] Donald and Deborah Leu outline the contents of a model Internet policy. They also provide websites where sample policies may be found. Acceptable-use policies are essential for gaining the best use of Internet resources among parents, students, and school staff.

Being Internet Savvy Helps You Help Students

Do you plan to help students learn a technology-based research process, and use other aspects of the Web to enhance their enthusiasm for books and reading? If so, you must acquire the skills yourself. Most students have few problems using computers, but they do have problems narrowing down their requests for information. The Internet can seem formidable for adults taking tentative steps into the world of cyberspace. To help you master these skills yourself, take a class, read a book, or learn from students, fellow teachers. You need to become proficient in using a web browsers and search engines, to locate addresses for websites you want to access.

If you do not have an URL (Uniform Resource Locators), but want to find information on a topic, there are other ways to connect to a website. There are now over 370 search engines on the web. The web page *www.whatis.com/Flat_Files/Search-Engines/0,282003,,00.html* explains what these are, and how to use them to your best advantage. Most library association websites have links to search engines they consider valuable. Traditional research techniques transfer readily to the Internet, so go ahead and explore. Remember, you can't get lost–click on "home," and you'll always get back to your starting point.

While adults often need encouragement to tackle the Internet, students usually do not hesitate before jumping in, but their willingness to push buttons can often lead them far afield. Most sites are not vocabulary controlled, and many have links to other sites not pertinent to the task at hand. These can be interesting time-wasters. Many websites are designed specifically for students, such as askjeeves.com, and you may wish to bookmark these.

Educational Time-Fillers

Websites often take a long time to load. This time can be used productively. Teachers and librarians may wish to assign these quick, reading-related fillers:

- Make a mental list of your favorite books and authors.

- Think of an author, and note all the books s/he has written.

- Pick an animal, and think of books in which this animal acts as a character, e.g., mice might lead to *Stuart Little* or *Ben and Me* or *Redwall*.

- Think of a number or color, and name as many books as you can with that number or color in the title, e.g. *The Book of Three.*

Pre-selected Sites

If you've found a site such as the "AskEricLessonPlans," which offers many lesson plans on a variety of subjects, at *http://www.askeric.org/Virtual/Lessons,* create a bookmark so you can go there instantly at a later time. You may wish to organize bookmarks into folders. It is a good idea to evaluate the websites you bookmark. Doug Johnson's article, "New Resources, New Selection Skills,"[2] suggests you evaluate sites in terms of the source's authority on the subject, content, vocabulary, timeliness, organization, and the links to other pages. It contains an excellent list of standards for website evaluation.

Advance planning helps ensure students are directed to the locations the librarian or teacher has determined to be most useful. You may wish to create a sample web page for students with the pertinent links. This will keep students on task and out of inappropriate sites, and will save time in the long run.

If you decide not to create your own web page, both of the two most popular search engines, Netscape Navigator and Internet Explorer, give you the opportunity to choose any web page as your own home page. The first screen to appear when students connect to the Internet will be a web browser. By pre-selecting the first site students will visit, you can make sure they'll get off to a successful start, as well as saving the time usually wasted when the home page for the browser is reproduced on the screen. Many schools now have their own web pages with appropriate links.

Once your pre-selected sites are checked, you can add Internet activities to your reading program. Students can look for web pages other schools have constructed. They can find information about the authors of books they are reading, about the books themselves, or find websites about the settings the author used. These can be used to construct timelines about the life experiences of authors, and see how these experiences have influenced their books. They can e-mail other schools or the authors themselves with their questions, and put on a contest of their own. Students can also help in designing a library web page for your library, where you can add current information about the contest activities and participating classrooms.

Just remember, the computer should be used to promote enthusiasm for reading, not as a substitute for reading. It shouldn't be used as a substitute for reading. In some schools, computers are seen not as a tool, but as an end in themselves. Esther Dyson, chairman of the Electronic Frontier Foundation, says "the issue is not education about computers, but computers as a means of education…"[3] Let's focus on the magic, but keep the robots in their place!

Great Sites for Librarians and Students

School Library Journal (January 2001, page 34) lists some of the "Best Sites For Media Specialists." This article, and this list of websites may be useful to you as you begin your planning.

1. **The Children's Literature Web Guide**
   www.acs.ucalgary.ca/~dkbrown/index.html
   Has links to many other websites, including a link to Kay Vandergrift's Special Interest Page — a fine collection of author webpages (at *www.scils.rutgers.edu/special/kay*).

2. **Kid's Search Tools**
   www.rcls.org/ksearch.html
   A selection of links to search tools for students and teachers.

3. **Notable Children's Websites**
   http://ala.org/alsc/ncwc.html
   Best websites for children ages birth–14.

4. **Brianna's Name That Book**
   http://members.home.net/ddays/books.html
   This site, compiled by homeschooler Brianna Day and her mother, is an excellent introduction to books and book contests.

5. **Oregon Authors Project**
   www.open.k12.or.us/ccp/authors
   Take a long look at this one. These are grade level reading tasks using various books and stories by Oregon authors.

6. **ACQWeb's Directory of Book Reviews on the Web**
   http://acqweb.library.vanderbilt.edu/acqweb/bookrev.html
   Useful links to reviewing journals in most curriculum fields.

7. **Reading, English and Communication: Great Web Resources**
   www.indiana.edu/~eric_rec/comatt/ghome.html
   Links to useful educational organizations.

8. **The Librarian's Guide to Cyberspace for Parents and Kids**
   www.ala.org/parentspage/greatsites/guide.html
   Amazing, spectacular, mysterious, colorful websites for kids and adults.

9. **Chris Brown's Virtual Reference Desk**
   www.virtualref.com
   A reference librarian's subject list of links to useful websites.

10. **Ask an Expert**
    http://askanexpert.com
    This is a "kid-friendly expert" site with hundreds of real-world experts, ranging from astronauts to zookeepers, available to answer student questions.

11. **Web Education**
    http://edweb.sdsu.edu/webquest/webquest.html
    This site is about teaching students to search the web for a purpose, and contains many lesson plans and tasks that can be used.

12. **Homework Help**
    http://school.discovery.com/homeworkhelp/bjpinchbeck
    A website designed and maintained by a middle grade student, who has

compiled lists of educational sites he has found useful.

13. **KidsClick Web Search**
    http://sunsite.berkeley.edu
    Developed by librarians, KidsClick guides young users to age appropriate websites divided by subject.

14. **Teachers Helping Teachers**
    www.pacificnet.net/~mandel/EducationalResources.html
    Provides educational links, lesson plans, book reviews and more.

15. **Children's Book Council Online Publishers Page**
    www.cbcbooks.org/navigation/pubindex.htm
    This carries author interviews and gives subject bibliography links to many author/illustrator sites.

16. **The Read In**
    www.readin.org/mainmenu.htm
    Contains names, pictures and information about current authors.

17. **The Multicultural Book Review Homepage**
    www.isomedia.com/homes/jmele/homepage.html
    Read reviews and submit your own reviews of multicultural books.

18. **KidsConnect**
    www.ala.org/ICONN/kidsconn.html
    A question-answering help and referral service designed by school librarians. It helps students access and use Internet information.

19. **Reading Zone of Internet Public Library**
    www.ipl.org/youth/ref.html
    Part of ipl.org. Students can ask questions of authors, get info., etc.

20. **The Academy Curriculum Exchange**
    http://ofcn.org/cyber.serv/academy/ace/lang/inter.html
    A variety of classroom lesson plans.

21. **Kathy Schrock's Guide for Educators**
    http://school.discovery.com/schrockguide
    An extensive list of technology resources to support and supplement almost any curriculum area.

22. **Librarians Information Online Network**
    www.libertynet.org/lion/bookmarks.html
    An excellent series of links to school librarians' oft-used information sources.

Endnotes

1. Leu, Donald J. and Deborah Diadian Leu. *Teaching with the Internet: Lessons from the Classroom.* Christopher Gordon, 1999.

2. Johnson, Doug. *The Indispensable Librarian.* Linworth ,1997, p. 22.

3. Dyson, Esther. "Symposium: the Reader in the Electronic Age." *Authors Guide Bulletin,* Winter 1997, p. 28.

Planning Saves Time

Advance planning is a life saver when reading activities begin, and everything happens at once. The more ducks you can line up ahead of time, the straighter your flight will be.

Planning will save time. As you read and think about what you want to do, jot down your ideas. Getting them written down is the first step.

Organization: Files Not Piles

The second step is organization. Find a cardboard box or plastic crate to create a project box that will hold a dozen or so file folders. Once you have the folders, you'll find you can do much preparation as you go about your daily library work. (Some may prefer to use a computer to organize their files, while others may find it's easier at this early stage to work with pencil and paper.) As you jot down ideas, notice references to contests, and find appropriate activities, drop the items into a folder, or add them to your computer file. (If you scribble a code on the item, such as "A" for activities, "B" for books, or "G" for goals, an aide can drop the items in the folder, saving more of your time.) When you actually start work on the project, much of the necessary preparation will already be completed and organized. We've provided some folder topics to get you started.

Folder 1: Goals and Reasons

When you introduce the idea to your administration and faculty, spell out exactly what you are going to do and why. Be prepared to answer such questions as "Why should we do this?", "How will this benefit the kids?", and "How will you measure its success?".

This folder is for notes on your own goals and any directives or suggestions from the state and/or district about the reading curriculum. You can also stash articles about reasons to and activities that encourage both students' reading and library involvement. This folder will provide the backup reasons for why you are spending time on these projects.

Folder 2: Reading Activities and Contests

This is where you can put information, rules, worksheets, and ideas on different methods to encourage reading. Notes on types of contests, different formats, and people or organizations who already sponsor these programs can go here. Scanning through your notes will help you decide on the format you'll use, as well as the procedures and rules that will work in your situation.

Folder 3: Books

As you scan your book shelves while helping students find books (or during library inventory), note some of the old favorites and overlooked titles. When new books come in, notes those that sound particularly useful. Lists of award-winning books and other bibliographies also go in this folder, especially those related to your own state award books. Award books are especially useful to include, because the award committees often supply supplementary publicity and activities.

Add any book suggestions from students and teachers, as well as clips from reviews and book catalogs. If you find a good website about authors and titles, note the website addresses. When the time comes to make up a book list, you'll find you already have a good start.

Folder 4: Questions

Sometimes, as you read reviews and catalog descriptions of books, you may find subjects for questions. Put these in this folder, along with sources of already prepared questions. Besides the questions we've included for our 250 chosen books, we've listed other sources in the bibliography.

Another time-saver for writing questions is to prepare question forms ahead of time and to keep those in this folder. These can also be created in the word processor "table" menu, or on a database or spreadsheet template.

Divide a standard sheet of paper into sixths. Put a place for author, title, and page number at the top of each section, and then "In which book…" should be written just below these. Keep your prepared sheets in this folder or as a computer template. You can use these sheets every time you write questions on a book, and they will remind you not to omit any pertinent information. Since they are standard size, they are ready to be used in your contests without retyping. Computer pages can be printed out as they are completed.

Folder 5: Cooperation with Others

Are you going to be working with other schools, districts, or other libraries? List the possibilities here. If other places or people will be involved, when will you need to contact them?

Find out which teachers are interested in becoming involved. Are any parents interested in helping? What classes will take part? How can you get the public library involved? How will you choose your teams? All ideas about these go into this folder.

Folder 6: Arrangements and Deadlines

This is for all the necessary odds and ends about setting up the contests. Where will the contests be held? Make sure you have access at the desired date and time. How will you set up the room? Teams should be grouped together around a table or in some way separated from the other teams. The audience should face the teams in comfortable seating. What chairs, tables, and timers will be needed?

Do you need a podium for the questioner? A seat near the teams for the time-keeper and scorekeeper, and judge?

Will you create a special shelf for the books, or mark the books in a special way, so they can be identified when on the shelf?

Note bulletin board ideas and other visual aids that can create interest. Also note ideas for team logos, badges, and awards.

Folder 7: Forms

Use your computer to create forms for anything you may repeat or modify later. Put a copy of each form you create in this folder, and make sure you put the file name and location on the copy. Otherwise, you may spend more time looking for a particular form than you did creating it in the first place!

Some useful forms are:

1. Book lists

2. Announcements for a school flyer

3. Announcements to teachers about contest times and places

4. Written rules for participants

5. List of books in bookmark format (could place on back of bookmark, p. 134)

6. Invitations for parents and school board members to attend

7. Certificates of Participation

8. Winners' certificates

9. Team identification logos and name tags

10. Score sheets (make sure there is room to tally the extra questions you use in case of tie scores)

Folder 8: Public Relations

Include copies of the newsletters you receive from the state, district, other schools and libraries. These are places you may wish to contact about what you are doing.

File copies of district news releases, since you may wish to copy the format. Add newspaper articles about school activities—these usually have bylines or department headings to contact for your own news releases. Include information about supplementary publicity and activities for award books.

Note the name of the school reporter for the local newspaper, the news anchor at the television station who does local news, and flyers and newsletters from places that might run publicity items, and any people who might be willing to photograph or video the contest.

If you're sponsoring a Battle of the Books through a public library or other agency, get a list of every school (public, religious, and independent) in your area, and file these names here. Make sure you have the names of every school board member and other movers and shakers in your community, so you can let them know what you are doing.

Folder 9: Timelines

When will you need to do what? Get a copy of the school calendar for this folder. If your school has special events coming up that will either conflict with or complement your contests, highlight these dates. As you think of things to do, pencil them in on this calendar. You might put in the dates when you need to prepare the book lists, invite people, arrange places, and introduce the idea to the students. When will the students begin forming teams? When will they get the lists and start reading books? When will the teams sign up?

Folder 10: Evaluations

Put a copy of your goals and objectives in this folder. You'll need this to evaluate how well these goals are met. Also use this for any written comments and suggestions you may receive—especially kudos!

Gather current statistics on student participation, circulation, and reading. Put in copies of the student reading scores from standardized tests. You can use these to gauge the project's impact.

Delegation

Computers

Computers are wonderful for dealing with all types of forms. Keep your book list on the computer. You can use this in future years, since you probably will carry over some, if not most, of the books. It's easy to insert and delete changes. You can also easily create bookmarks with titles and authors.

Some librarians like to save questions in a computer file. If you write your questions by hand on standard size paper or file cards as you are reading the books, you may find retyping is unnecessary. Just work with your hand-written cards. If you're sharing with others, then use the computer. Others can type in the questions for you.

Computers are also helpful in sorting items by different subjects. You can create book lists on any subject by using your database and creating subject, grade level, or other fields. Use a year field in the book list file, and you will know in which years you used certain titles.

E-mail

If you get e-mail from a variety of people and places, you can have your mailbox sort items into different folders for you. You can set up one for all e-mail from LM_NET (the library media specialists' discussion list), one for mail from the administration, and one for all correspondence in relation to the Battle of the Books. If you don't know how mail can be sorted, locate the instructions on the help screen in your computer. Using these tools can save an amazing amount of time.

Other Librarians and Teachers

If you team up with other librarians to conduct the Battle of the Books, you can also share the question-writing. You can divide the books to be used, write the questions on just those books, and e-mail them to the others. Teachers can also be persuaded to write questions on their favorite books. You will need one person to review all these questions for accuracy and to make sure they can't be answered by more than one title. This person must be someone who has read all the books.

Volunteers

You can't delegate the question typing to students, but you can use students for other typing and filing tasks. Students can write questions, promote the program to other students, create bookmarks and bulletin board displays, and write book reviews. They may also enjoy creating web pages with links to the battle books and their authors.

Parents can type questions, locate teaching guides and author information on the Internet, record books on tape, and read books aloud to students. They can also prepare purchase orders for videos, books on tape, and teacher guides for battle books.

Both can clip articles from catalogs, and file the items you think you may need in the appropriate folders. This is where using folders is helpful; they can be worked on whenever free time is available.

Remember that what saves time for one person may not work for another. For example, some articles about time-saving tips suggest doing two things at once. Others point out that people who do two things at once are doubly lucky—they get to do everything twice! Try these ideas if you like. Ask around. You may find other time-savers that work for you.

Preparing for Battle

Since encouraging the love of reading is at the heart of all book contests, the book selection process is critical. Choose books that offer something to think and talk about, and which help students understand the people and events that make up our world.

The book lists you prepare will not only be used by students, but are often used as selection aids by teachers, parents, and other members of the community. The books we have chosen to include in this manual are suitable for the middle school, usually grades 6–8. Some books for these students have themes and language that are appropriate for independent reading, but may not be suitable for reading aloud to a classroom. Make sure you, or another reliable adult has read each book before putting it on the list, and make sure that teachers read them in advance before reading them aloud.

Choosing the Books

You want to include a wide variety of books, including prize winners, new books, and traditional or modern classics. Include a variety of genres, so students will have a chance to read different types of books. Consider length, reading level difficulty, and theme. Solicit suggestions for the books from teachers, students, and other librarians.

Most state library associations annually honor outstanding children's or young adult books. These titles make excellent choices for your list. School districts often have recommended or required reading lists. California has a list of recommended books for all their school libraries, and other states have similar lists.[1]

Students need to feel successful, so start with the easier and more familiar books. Harder ones can be added later. Although you want books that have some depth to them, they do not have to be difficult books.

Inventory time is a good time to note books currently being overlooked by students and teachers. Stick a marker on the spine of these not-to-be-forgotten titles. Add some of these to next year's list. This is a way of bringing these "golden oldies" to everyone's attention. Sometimes the discovery of an overlooked author or title will lead children to read other books by the same author or in the same genre.

Make sure you have enough copies of each title to meet your needs. This will depend on the size of the list, as well as the number of participants. A program using a small list to serve a large group of students will need several copies of each title; a large list or small student group may need only one or two copies of each book.

Schools vary in the number of books they use. Much depends on the type of competition, the number of students who participate, and the library's collection of books. Some schools use as few as 10 titles at a time, while others may use up to 100.

The Des Plaines School District (Illinois) begins with 10 books in the first November round; they add another 10 books in January, another 10 in February, and still another 10 in March.[2]

Since many of the same students participate every year, you will need to change the list of books from one year to the next. If you don't change, the more experienced students will have an edge. With 100 books on a list, at least a third of these should be changed annually. A smaller book list may need to be totally revised. Be sure to keep track of the titles used each year. A computerized database will help you keep track of book titles and the years in which they appear on the list.

Writing the Questions

After choosing the books you're going to use, read them with paper and pencil in hand. Look for incidents and characters that are distinctive and interesting. Stick a slip of paper in each page with such a topic. Questions can be sketched out on these for later revision, and it's a good idea to note the page numbers before you remove the card from the book. This helps if someone challenges the question.

Use a separate slip of paper for each question. Make up a form you can run off, use index cards, or create a template in a word processor or database. Make sure you write the name of the author, title of the book, and page number on each slip—you may find yourself forgetting these under pressure!

With a large list of books, you will need a minimum of four or five questions for each book. This will give you some to use during regular battles, plus one or two harder ones to keep in reserve for playoffs. If you have a small book list, you will need to have more questions. You can reuse questions, but if the same one is used too often, some students will begin to memorize the answers. Alaska uses 72 questions per book—24 for the practices, 24 for the district competition, and 24 for the state competition. That is a lot of questions to prepare!

Most of the questions included in this book are knowledge and comprehension questions, which rely on memory. These are simple in structure. They can test students' general knowledge of a book, and they can be answered by almost anyone who has read the book. To help students keep track of the details of the books they read, you can include a "Fact Tracker" bookmark with every Battle title. This form allows students to record relevant information as they read. (See p. 135 for pattern.)

There are several guidelines to follow in creating questions. Vary the content. You want this to be an enjoyable project, not a test, so try to avoid tricky questions. You may wish to include a few "giveaway" questions in your first few battles. These give students confidence. Surprisingly, some questions which seem to be too easy actually turn out to be stumpers. If you make questions too easy or too vague, they may apply to more than one book.

Questions can be related to setting, character, plot, or theme. They can range from a very broad topic in the book, to a very specific question on an event. Avoid using direct quotations which are used only once in a book—but repeated quotations, such as Gurgi's "crunching and munchings" in Alexander's Prydain books, can be used to good effect.

Make the questions interesting by using colorful and memorable details. Don't use questions that give away the book's ending. You'll find that your questions often sell a particular book to the audience—another side benefit of the program.

Questions should be fairly short. If they are too wordy, students may forget the beginning of the question by the time you get to the end. The vocabulary used in the question should be appropriate to the grade level of the students and should reflect the vocabulary used in the book. As questions are used and reused, you may naturally rephrase them to fit your own speaking patterns. Watch this though: sometimes a simple change or omission can make the question apply to another title.

Although the questions need to be brief, sometimes brevity or paraphrasing can cause a problem by not properly representing the particular book. *Reread all questions before using them!*

Questions need to be very specific and to fit only one book on the list. Sometimes you may need to use a character's name in order to make the question apply to a particular book. It's usually best, however, to avoid using such names, especially if they form part of the title of the book. Use such generic terms such as "heroine," "boy," or "main character," Though gender references also give a strong clue.

It's difficult to write questions that are specific to a particular book of nonfiction. There are many books on World War II, and they often refer to the same incidents. This can also be true of fiction books about the subject.

Biography can also be tricky. Questions about Lewis and Clark, for example, can apply to several versions. If you use these, make sure you have a question or two that can be answered only from the version you have decided to use. You can always make questions apply to your own particular title by beginning the question with "In which book on our list.." instead of "In which book..."

Watch out for questions that can be answered by reading the brief annotations on catalog cards, book jackets, or online. Online bookstores often have annotations and/or fairly extensive reviews. Make sure questions are based on the original book, rather than a video version, which might have different incidents and characters.

Avoid the trivial question which really doesn't matter to the story. For example, clothing is generally unimportant. On the other hand, some articles of clothing are quite distinctive to a character, such as Sam Gribley's rabbit skin underwear,[3] which can make a good question.

During the contest time, look at the missed and challenged questions. Sometimes you can spot a confusing phrase or ambiguity. If you think the question is still a good one, reuse it in a later battle. Place a checkmark on the used questions, so you don't repeat them too often. As you continue to work with the program, you will find yourself modifying questions and creating your own to suit your own style and your own students.

Analyzing questions submitted by others also involves higher-order thinking skills. Inviting students to create their own questions also encourages these skills. Usually, students enjoy writing questions for other battles. For example, some Urbana (Illinois) students decided to create a battle for their teachers. They wrote all the questions for this with the help of their public librarians. Writing questions can supplement the usual book reports as a classroom assignment, if the teacher approves.

If you decide to include student-created questions, keep a "question suggestion" box available in the library. You may need to demonstrate how to create questions that only apply to a particular book. Point out that not all questions submitted will be used. You will have to edit all questions for clarity, grammar and specifics, and verify that the questions are based on the book rather than a video version. Insist that all questions include title, author, and page number of the book, as well as the name of the person submitting it.

Make sure you give verbal credit during the battles to the originator of those questions which are used. Identical or similar questions are often submitted by students, since the same incident or character often appeals to different readers. In this case, the first person to submit the question receives the credit.

The above rules are only guidelines for writing questions. They are not as overwhelming as they seem. Once you have established an original core of books and questions, you'll find it fairly easy to keep up with year-to-year additions. If you send a query to LM_NET, you will find many other librarians who are usually more than happy to share questions. The questions you create yourself, aimed at your own particular students, will be the ones you will prefer using. It really is fun to go through the books, selecting the parts that seem most vivid to you, while also thinking of individual students who will be wrestling with the questions you are writing!

Setting Up the Battles

Set the place, the time, and choose your participants. Once teams are chosen, they will begin to work together. It's interesting to see how students organize their preparation. Some read only the books on the list that interest them, and don't worry about anything else. Other groups become very organized, and assign each team member a certain number of titles. Some students spend their lunch hours exchanging comments about the books, and then quizzing each other. In some cases, a team may consist of a single student; in 1999, such a student from Chicken, Alaska, was one of that state's champion teams.

At least three people are needed for the actual battles. You'll need a timer—someone to watch the clock and signal when a team's time is up. You need a quiz master to read the questions to the teams. An accurate scorekeeper is also necessary. You may also want to have a judge, other than the questioner, to rule on challenges. These are all good ways to involve any adult or student volunteer in the audience.

Make sure your room is set up to allow the audience to see the team members—and that the questions in the quiz master's hands are not viewable by students. Before the contest, congratulate the team members for their reading and hard work. This is a good time to hand out participation certificates, if you are using them. Afterwards, take a lead from the P. E. department and have members of opposing teams shake hands with one another.

Rules

You need to decide on the rules for the Battle of the Books contests, and let students and teachers know them in advance. These can be included with the book lists given students. The following rules work for our schools; look them over and make any changes you feel necessary:

1. Any group of four students may form a team and challenge any other team by making arrangements with the library staff. Friends should not sign up a student without the student's knowledge and approval. No changes in membership can be made to a team once it has been formed.

2. Each team is made up of four players. If a member is absent, the remaining players play as a team with no substitutes.

3. There are 20 questions to a game.

4. Each team has 30 seconds to come up with the correct answer. They may confer with each other if they wish. During that 30 seconds, they may have as many guesses as they like, and anyone on the team may speak.

5. Questions may be asked on any of the books on the given list, but on no other books.

6. The team receives five points for each correct title, and three points if they can give the correct name of the author, for a possible total of eight points per question.

7. If, at the end of 30 seconds, the team is unable to answer the question, the opposing team has five seconds in which to give the correct answer. They have only one chance. If they miss, the question goes to the audience.

8. If the first team is able to give the title of the book (and scores five points), but cannot name the author, the opposing team does not have a chance to answer the question for the additional three points.

9. The audience may not coach members of the team, or talk while the battle is going on. When a question is missed by both teams, the audience may answer any part of the question, either author or title, that has not been answered by either team.

10. All students must remain in their seats at all times.

Scoring

If you are using 10 rounds of questions per team, take a break after five questions and announce the half-time score.

How many points will students receive for answering the questions correctly? You might be very simple and give one point for each correct title, and another for each correct author. A bonus point can be added if both parts of the question are answered. Most schools give five points for a correct title, and three points for the correct rendition of the author's name.

Create score sheets to be used for the battles. Use a form with room for 20 questions. This makes it easy to check the answers in the appropriate column as each team takes their turn. If the question is not answered, the corresponding column is left blank. It's then very simple to tally the total points at the end.

You also need to decide how much time you will give students to respond. Usually 30 seconds is enough time for students to come up with the answer. If a team misses the question, the question goes to the other team. They have only five seconds to come up with the answer since they have already heard this question.

Tournaments and Playoffs

Tournaments add to the competitive excitement. They also make a good end-of-year activity. Middle school students usually understand the concept of "seeding" teams according to their average scores. This keeps interest high, as teams which are roughly equivalent in ability progress through a series of "brackets" until a winner is chosen. Seeding keeps the best teams from eliminating each other in early rounds, since they don't meet until the very end.

If you use this method, you will need to have an even number of teams. Don't use more than 16, though, or it will take forever! You can have some preliminary play-off battles if it is necessary to eliminate a team or two in order to get down to 16.

The next step is to determine the average score for each team, by adding up their total scores and dividing by the number of battles they played. Rank each team in descending order.

Divide the number of teams in half to get a number that you will use to separate the teams. For example, if you have 16 teams, this number will be eight. If there are 10 teams, the number will be five. This is the number that will be used to match the teams as you place them in the brackets. This keeps the pairings relatively even.

Ask a school coach for one of the bracket charts often furnished to the athletic department, or use the sample below. Arrange your teams within the brackets. Brackets are arranged by putting each pair of teams within a bracket. Begin by working with the odd-numbered teams. Repeat the process for the even numbered teams. These examples can be adapted to any number of teams that you have. Eight or 16 teams work out evenly, and make it easy to figure. However, if you keep the method of separating the teams in mind, you should be able to work out the brackets for any number of teams in the finals. "Byes" can be used when there are unequal numbers of teams. Another method of handling unequal numbers is to let the losing team with the best score be in the quarter or semi-finals.

If you divide the number of teams by the number of battles you plan for a given day, you will come up with the number of days you will need for the final tournament. With three battles on a given day, the playoffs for 16 teams will take five days to complete. At three battles a day, the playoffs will take four days to complete.

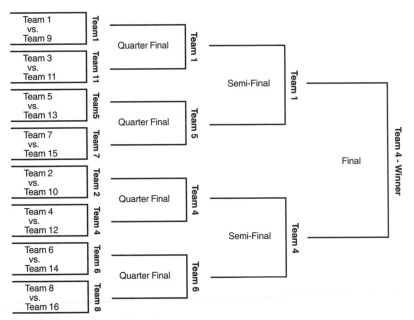

Sample bracket chart for 16-team tournament play-off

Public Relations

Here is a list of suggestions for public relations for your Battle of the Books. You may wish to do everything, or just choose a few.

- Prepare colorful bulletin boards to attract attention to the battles. If you can, use the bulletin boards in the school's front hall, so all visitors to the school will know about the program.

- Talk up the activity beforehand. Book talk some of the titles on your list—but just give teasers of the plot.

- Write articles for newsletters and the local paper, or let the English classes do these—it's good writing practice.

- Put out a special monthly newsletter for each grade. These cover books and magazines, what classes are doing, and library activities. They are printed on bright paper and sent home to parents.

- If you have a library or school newsletter about activities, route copies to every library in your region, the administrators in the district, and all school board members. The latter are usually given packets before their monthly meetings; see if your newsletter can be placed in these packets.

- If you are using e-mail to compete with schools in other districts, make sure the local media knows. Anything with technology seems to have great appeal!

- Prepare special invitations that students can take home to their parents. Send invitations to all district administrators.

- Arrange for a video camera, and any other publicity you may wish to have.

Evaluation

At the end of the school year, when you are returning books to the regular collection, tally any evidence of increased circulation in the books placed on the list. Gather statistics on student participation, circulation, and reading.

As you plan for the following year, you may wish to survey teachers and students. How can you make the program better next year? Solicit suggestions for improvements from all participants: parents, teachers, students, and any others who may have been involved. Their reactions to the project are invaluable in making sure that the program continues to meet their expectations, and justifies your time and effort.

Some of the topics you may wish to cover are: did the teachers get new ideas for classroom read-alouds? Do they feel students improved their leisure time reading habits and reading skills? Were there any improvements in scores on standardized tests?

Remember, your main purpose is to encourage the love of reading. All participants need to have a feeling of success, not failure. Don't let the idea of school playoffs, winners, or test scores become the focus of the program. You really do want students to feel that this is one of the best activities they've ever done!

Endnotes

1. Lists of these usually can be obtained from your state library association. Charlotte Huck's book, *Children's Literature in the Elementary School, 6th edition,* (McGraw-Hill,1996) gives the addresses of most award committees in Appendix A. Dolores Blyth Jones lists winners in *Children's Literature Awards and Winners: A Directory of Prizes, Authors and Illustrators, 2nd edition,* (Gale Research, 1994). Another list of present and past winners can be found in *Children's Books: Awards and Prizes,* which may be obtained from the Children's Book Council, 67 Irving Place, New York, NY 10003.

2. "Presenting Battle of the Books," (District #62, Des Plaines, Illinois, 1980, photocopy.)

3. George, Jean. *My Side of the Mountain.* Dutton, 1959.

About the Books and Questions

Middle school students are beginning the transition from childhood to adulthood. They are becoming aware of society's problems, and are interested in finding answers. Everyone knows that reading levels vary widely. So do maturity levels. Some students are still functioning in the comfort of childhood, while others are physically mature and/or are expected to take on adult responsibilities.

Students possess varied backgrounds and experience. Some have read and traveled widely and are acquainted with different groups of people. Other have little first-hand experience with anything outside their immediate family, school, and town.

A Varied Selection

Choosing books for this age represents a challenge. We have attempted to include a variety of genres and levels, so you can pick and choose those most appropriate for your own library and students.

There are books for most reading levels, from easy books like Naylor's *Shiloh* to such books as *Ishi*, written at an adult level. Most books have been listed on various "best books" lists, and many have won honors. Some books that need little reading experience to enjoy them, such as Clement's *Frindle*. Others, like Pullman's *The Golden Compass*, will benefit from some knowledge of background settings. Yolen's *Briar Rose*, is for students who have read widely and can comprehend how this innocuous fairy tale is used as a framework for a story of the Nazi death camps.

Prereading and Prescreening is Essential

It is *very* important to read the books before using them. All "Battle" books gain the status of assigned books. Some of the books on our list cover mature themes. Most of these will be remembered by readers. They portray hope for the character's future. Award-winner Chris Crutcher's *Stotan*, for example, portrays the bonding among members of a swim team, and how this bonding helps the characters deal with life problems. The teenage language and the portrayal of the battering father, however, may not be suitable for immature readers. Some parents are uncomfortable with these types of books, because they may believe that reading about a topic is the same as teaching a topic.

There are many awards given to well-written books. Most of the books on our list have won one or more awards, and have been listed in many bibliographies, such as the ALA Notable Books. We cannot note every award. Since the Newbery list seems to be a touchstone for librarians and teachers, and the Coretta Scott King Award is useful for diversity, we have noted only these two. We are using the words "Newbery" and "Coretta Scott King" to refer to both the award book and the Honor Books. You'll find these books listed in the "Awards" line of this booklist.

The ISBN number is included in the publication line. As publishers merge and acquire imprints, and as books go into other editions, ISBNs can differ. Classics such as *Treasure Island* are available in many different editions. We have tried to include the most widely available version, whether hard cover or paperback. Check the online bookstores for the latest updates.

Many books are available in video or audio formats. Since the reason for Battle of the Books is to encourage reading, these are not mentioned. We have, however, noted some available study guides and websites, since these are inexpensive and can increase knowledge of the author, the book, and its content.

Websites are listed in the "URL" line. These URLs, or Universal Resource Locators, are supposed to take you directly to a useful website. The ones listed were current as of January, 2001, but by the time you read this, many will have moved or disappeared. Kay Vandergrift and David Brown both do a good job of keeping up with changes (see their websites listed in chapter 4), and publishers frequently have links to their authors' websites and even lesson plans. Using search sites like Yahoo and Yahooligans will provide you with other connections.

Many companies also publish teachers guides for books. We have noted those we have found, and used an abbreviation for them. See the chart below for a list of abbreviations and ordering information.

Abbreviation	Series Name	Publisher
Connect*	Connect Books	Sundance Publishing P.O. Box 1326 Littleton, MA 01460
LEAP*	Literature Enrichment Activities for Paperbacks	Sundance Publishing, P.O. Box 1326 Littleton, MA 01460
LIFT*	Literature is for Thinking	Sundance Publishing P.O. Box 1326 Littleton, MA 01460
Lit. U.	Literature Units	Teacher Created Materials 6421 Industry Way Westminster, CA 92683.
LL	Novel-Ties	Learning Links 1300 Marcus Ave. New Hyde Park, NY 11042.
Novel Units*	Novel Units	Mari, Inc. 1025 25th St. Santa Monica, CA 90403.
Portals*	Portals to Reading	Perfection Learning 1000 N 2nd Ave. Logan, IA 51546-1061.
RBB*	Reading Beyond the Basals	Sundance Publishing P.O. Box 1326 Littleton, MA 01460
Sch.	Scholastic Literature Guides	Scholastic, Inc. 555 Broadway New York, NY 10012-3999.

* All starred items can be ordered from Mari, Inc., 1025 25th St., Santa Monica, CA 90403.

Battle Books and Questions

Across Five Aprils

Irene Hunt. Viking, 1942. ISBN 0-8136-7202-3.
URL: www.sunsite.utk.edu/civil-war/
    www.civilwar.com
Awards: Newbery
Study Guides: LL; Portals
Subjects: historical fiction—Civil War

Questions

1. In which book are the loyalties of a border state family divided between the North and the South during the Civil War?

2. In which book does an angry Union mob burn a barn and put coal oil in a well?

3. In which book does an Illinois farm boy get in trouble because his brother has joined the Rebel army?

4. In which book do the "cracker barrel heroes" pick on Jethro when he defends a southern soldier?

5. In which book does Dave Burdow, a family's enemy, protect their youngest son from an attack?

Across the Wide and Lonesome Prairie: The Oregon Trail Diary of Hattie Campbell

Kristiana Gregory. Scholastic, 1997. ISBN 0-590-22651-7.
URL: www.pbs.org/opb/oregontrail/teacher/popcharts.html
Subjects: historical fiction

Questions

1. In which book does a father decide to move to Oregon after his brother's coffin slides into the Mississippi River?

2. In which book is baby River Anne Valentine born during a river crossing?

3. In which book do some children die from eating water hemlock, picked by a girl who thought it was parsnip?

4. In which book does a woman steal things from other families on the wagon train?

5. In which book is a bride's wedding dress made from a lace tablecloth?

The Adventures of Tom Sawyer

Mark Twain. Puffin,1995. ISBN 0-140366733.
URL: www.marktwain.about.com/arts/marktwain/
Study Guides: LL
Subjects: classic

Questions

1. In which book does a boy trick his friends into whitewashing a fence by pretending it's fun?

2. In which book do two boys see a murder in a graveyard?

3. In which book does a boy let himself be whipped to protect the person who actually tore the teacher's book?

4. In which book do rescuers board up a cave after finding some lost children, without realizing the robbers are still inside?

5. In which book does a boy hope the schoolmaster will punish him so that he can sit with the girls?

Afternoon of the Elves

Janet Lisle. Orchard, 1989. ISBN 0-531-08437-X (hc); ISBN 0-590-43944-8 (pb).
URL: www.janettaylorlisle.com/author.htm
Awards: Newbery
Subjects: fantasy

Questions

1. In which book does an eleven-year-old girl secretly care for her mother all by herself?

2. In which book does a girl make a tiny village in her backyard?

3. In which book does a miniature Ferris wheel made from bicycle wheels begin to turn by itself?

4. In which book does a character risk losing her old friends because of her fascination with the strange girl living behind her?

5. In which book is a character teased for bringing only cereal for her school lunch?

Alanna: The First Adventure

Tamora Pierce. Atheneum, 1983. ISBN 0-614-28945-9 (pb).
URL: www.sff.net/people/Tamora.Pierce/
Subjects: fantasy; strong female

Questions

1. In which book does a girl take her brother's place in training to become a knight?

2. In which book does a new page in a castle win a fight with an older and larger bully?

3. In which book does a girl with the gift of healing discover that her power is much stronger than she had known?

4. In which book does a young character find a magic sword in the ruins of an ancient stronghold?

5. In which book is a sorcerer suspected of being the prince's enemy?

Alice's Adventures in Wonderland

Lewis Carroll. Dutton, 1998. ISBN 0-525-46094-2.
URL: http://falcon.jmu.edu/~ramseyil/carroll.htm
Subjects: classic; fantasy

Questions

1. In which book does a girl change her size by eating and drinking different things?

2. In which book does a blue caterpillar tell a story about Father William?

3. In which book does a character fall down a rabbit hole?

4. In which book does a character swim in a pool of tears?

5. In which book is a croquet game played with live flamingos and hedgehogs?

...and now Miguel

Joseph Krumgold. Crowell, 1953. ISBN 0-690-09118-4 (hc); ISBN 0-06-440143-X (pb).
URL: www.readingacrossusa.com/book0215.htm
Awards: Newbery
Subjects: historical fiction

Questions

1. In which book does a boy fool a ewe into adopting an orphan lamb?

2. In which book is a family glad when the Marquez brothers come to shear their sheep?

3. In which book does a character try to undo a prayer after his brother is drafted into the army?

4. In which book is a character called "a real pastor" after he skips school in order to find the family's lost sheep?

5. In which book does someone pray to San Ysidro for the chance to journey to the Sangre de Cristo mountains?

Angry Waters

Walt Morey. Blue Heron, 1990. ISBN 0-936-08510-X.
URL: www.pcez.com/~hobbit/morey.htm
Subjects: adventure; contemporary issues

Questions

1. In which book is a character sent to work on a farm as a condition of his probation?

2. In which book is a character arrested for driving a car during a supermarket holdup?

3. In which book does Dan stand off a calf-killing cougar?

4. In which book does a character train two calves, Rosie and Beauty?

5. In which book does a character's knowledge of motors prove useful in salvaging logs from the Columbia River?

Anne of Green Gables

Lucy M. Montgomery. Puffin, 1994. ISBN 0-14-0367411.
URL: www.upei.ca/~lmmi/core.html
Study Guides: Portals; Lit. U.; Novel Units
Subjects: classic; families

Questions

1. In which book does a character refuse to speak to someone for five years because he teased her when she first came to the school?

2. In which book does a girl almost drown when she floats down river on a flatboat while pretending to be Elaine of Astolat?

3. In which book does a redhead break a slate over the head of her tormentor?

4. In which book are orphan children expected to work for their keep?

5. In which book does a character break an ankle after accepting a dare to walk on the ridge of a roof?

The Apprenticeship of Lucas Whitaker

Cynthia DeFelice. Farrar Straus Giroux, 1996. ISBN 0-374-34669-0.
URL: www.powells.com/biblio/24800-25000/0374346690.html
Subjects: historical fiction

Questions

1. In which book does a doctor insist scientists must test theories over and over to see "if they keep true"?

2. In which book does an orphan find a home by working for a doctor?

3. In which book does a character insist winter baths are healthy?

4. In which book do rumors about cures for consumption travel quickly over mountains and valleys?

5. In which book does a boy learn about healing plants from an old Indian woman?

Armageddon Summer

Jane Yolen and Bruce Coville. Harcourt Brace, 1998. ISBN 00-15-201767-4 (hc); ISBN 0-15-202268-6 (pb).
URL: www.ipl.org/youth/AskAuthor/Yolen.html
    www.janeyolen.com
Notes: This book may offend some groups.
Subjects: contemporary issues

Questions

1. In which book do two characters meet on a mountainside while they wait for the world to end?

2. In which book is 144 an important number?

3. In which book does a character conceal a laptop computer because it is considered a tool of the devil?

4. In which book is an old volume of poems by Emily Dickinson the only birthday present someone receives?

5. In which book is a church encampment fortified and guarded to keep campers in and others out?

The Ballad of Lucy Whipple

Karen Cushman. Houghton Mifflin, 1996. ISBN 0-395-72806-1.
URL: www.ipl.org/youth/AskAuthor/cushmanbio.html
    http://harperchildrens.com/schoolhouse/TeachersGuides/cushmanindex.htm
Study Guides: Novel Units
Subjects: historical fiction

Questions

1. In which book does a girl change her name because she does not like California?

2. In which book does a girl write letters to her grandparents complaining about life in a mining camp?

3. In which book does a character earn money by selling pies?

4. In which book does a character start a lending library with a box of books from her old home?

5. In which book does a character give her father's name to a runaway slave?

Bandit's Moon

Sid Fleischman. Greenwillow, 1998. ISBN 0-688-15830-7-0.
URL: www.carr.lib.md.us/authco/fleischman.htm
Subjects: historical fiction; strong female

Questions

1. In which book is someone rescued by outlaws from an old woman who is holding the character prisoner?

2. In which book does a character teach the captor to read by using an old recipe book?

3. In which book does a character refuse to name a horse for fear of becoming attached to him?

4. In which book does an outlaw laugh at a poster advertising a price on his head?

5. In which book is the character's brother falsely reported to have been killed by a famous outlaw?

Bat 6

Virginia Euwer Wolff. Scholastic, 1998. ISBN 0-590-89799-3.
URL: www.scholastic.com/titles/bat6.htm
Subjects: historical fiction; prejudice

Questions

1. In which book does each of the characters from Barlow Ridge and Beaver Creek schools tell the story from his or her own point of view?

2. In which book do two new students in town become the best players on the teams?

3. In which book does the unreasoning prejudice a child learned as a baby cause her to hurt someone else?

4. In which book do the women plan a baseball game to get the men of two towns talking to one another?

5. In which book does a Japanese-American girl try to forget all the Japanese words that she knows?

Beauty

Bill Wallace. Holiday, 1988. ISBN 0-671-74188-8 (pb).
Subjects: animals

Questions

1. In which book does a character discover the difference between riding a cattle horse and a trail horse?

2. In which book must a character shoot a beloved horse after her legs get caught in a cattle guard?

3. In which book does a gentle mother strike a neighbor because she thinks he has been starving her horse?

4. In which book is a character talked into playing cowboy with the horses after his grandfather tells him "No"?

5. In which book does a grandfather catch his leg in a hay baler?

Belle Prater's Boy

Ruth White. Farrar Straus Giroux, 1996. ISBN 0-374-30668-0 (hc); ISBN 0-440-41372-9 (pb).
URL: www.carr.lib.md.us/authco/white.htm
    www.randomhouse.com/teachers/guides/bell.html
Awards: Newbery
Study Guides: Portals; Lit. U.; Novel Units; LEAP; LIFT; RBB
Subjects: contemporary issues

Questions

1. In which book does a character move from Crooked Ridge to his grandparents' home in town after his mother disappears?

2. In which book is a character teased for being cross-eyed?

3. In which book does a very proper lady roll up her skirts to wade in the creek at a tea party?

4. In which book does a girl cut her long, lovely hair because she feels that it hides her real self?

5. In which book is a character frightened by a dark shape that is seen often in a nightmare?

Beyond the Western Sea Book 1: The Escape from Home

Avi. Orchard, 1996. ISBN 0-531-08863-4 (hc).
URL: www.carr.org/read/fiction.htm
        www.avi-writer.com/
Subjects: historical fiction; immigrants

Questions

1. In which book do the main characters receive tickets to sail from Ireland to America?

2. In which book does a character from a wealthy family run away from home after a harsh beating from his elder brother?

3. In which book are travelers deceived by a disreputable gang known as the Lime Street Runners Association?

4. In which book does a Catholic child worry when befriended by a clergyman of Protestant faith?

5. In which book does a character stow away in a crate of hats marked with a cross in a circle?

The Black Stallion

Walter Farley. Random House. ISBN 0-394-90601-2 (hc); ISBN 0-590-31564-1 (pb).
URL: www.venice-florida.com/Community/Education/farley.htm
Study Guides: Portals; Lit. U.; Novel Units; LEAP
Subjects: animals

Questions

1. In which book does a horse save a character from losing his life?

2. In which book does Alec insist that his rescue ship must also rescue his horse?

3. In which book do a character and a horse travel by ship from India to New York?

4. In which book does the character land with a horse on an uninhabited island after they are shipwrecked?

5. In which book does a wild stallion race at last in the Kentucky Derby?

The Blossoms and the Green Phantom

Betsy Byars. Delacorte, 1987. ISBN 0-385-29533-2 (hc); ISBN 0-440-40069-4 (pb).
URL: www.randomhouse.com/catalog/display.pperl?isbn=0440400694
Subjects: contemporary issues; families

Questions

1. In which book is helium used for a special invention?

2. In which book does a character feel he's a failure because none of his many inventions has ever worked?

3. In which book is a grandfather trapped inside a dumpster when he tries to rescue a puppy?

4. In which book is a dog called "Mud" jealous of "Dump?"

5. In which book does a character invent something from three air mattresses and some garbage bags?

The Boggart

Susan Cooper. Aladdin, 1995. ISBN 0-689-80173-4 (pb).
URL: www.puffin.co.uk/living/aut_10.html
Subjects: contemporary issues; fantasy

Questions

1. In which book does a Canadian family inherit a castle on MacDevon's Island in Scotland?

2. In which book does an iron lock block a magician's escape?

3. In which book does a character's ability to read Gaelic direct the main characters' actions?

4. In which book is an old piece of furniture sent from Scotland to Canada with an unexpected passenger inside?

5. In which book do theater and traffic lights inexplicably flicker and change color?

The Book of Three

Lloyd Alexander. Holt, 1964. ISBN 0-8050-6132-0 (hc); ISBN 0-440-91069-2 (pb).
URL: www.cbcbooks.org/navigation/autindex.htm
      www.penguinputnam.com/cgi-
bin/to_catalog.cgi?section=catalog&page=yreader/authors/2235_biography.html
Subjects: fantasy

Questions

1. In which book does a character find adventure when Hen Wen the pig runs away?

2. In which book does a boy live with a 379-year-old enchanter?

3. In which book is a character freed from a dungeon by mistake?

4. In which book does a princess rescue someone from a dungeon?

5. In which book is there a hairy character who always wants some "crunchings and munchings?"

Briar Rose

Jane Yolen. Tor, 1992. ISBN 0-812-55862-6.
URL: www.ipl.org/youth/AskAuthor/Yolen.html
    www.janeyolen.com
Subjects: historical fiction—World War II; contemporary issues; prejudice

Questions

1. In which book does Gemma tell her granddaughters the story of Sleeping Beauty?

2. In which book does a grandmother use a fairy tale to describe how she survived the Holocaust?

3. In which book is a woman rescued from a pit of corpses?

4. In which book does a character discover the story of her grandparents?

5. In which book does a character inherit a wooden box with a rose on the lid containing mysterious photographs and newspaper clippings?

Bridge to Terabithia

Katherine Paterson. Harper, 1977. ISBN 0-690-01359-0 (hc); ISBN 0-06-440184-7 (pb).
URL: www.ipl.org/youth/AskAuthor/paterson.html
    www.terabithia.com/
Awards: Newbery
Study Guides: LL; Portals; Lit. U.; Novel Units; LEAP; RBB; Sch.
Subjects: contemporary issues; grief and death

Questions

1. In which book is a character out-raced by a new fifth-grader?

2. In which book do two characters use Narnia as a pattern for their own private world?

3. In which book does a character's best friend fall off a rope into a flooded stream?

4. In which book is a character befriended by the music teacher?

5. In which book does a boy share his own private world with his little sister, after the death of his best friend?

The Bronze Bow

Elizabeth Speare. Houghton Mifflin, 1961. ISBN 0-395-87769-5 (hc); ISBN 0-395-13719-5 (pb).
URL: www.penncharter.com/student/israel/index.html
    www.indiana.edu/~eric_rec/ieo/bibs/speare.html
Awards: Newbery
Study Guides: LL; Novel Units
Subjects: historical fiction

Questions

1. In which book does a deaf/mute save another character's life?

2. In which book is the title taken from the password used by a band of rebels?

3. In which book does a character decide to become a blacksmith and to look after his sister Leah?

4. In which book do some children pledge to fight against the Romans?

5. In which book is a character part of an outlaw band fighting the Roman conquerors?

Bud, Not Buddy

Christopher Paul Curtis. Delacorte, 1999. ISBN 0-385-32306-9.
URL: http://falcon.jmu.edu/~ramseyil/curtis.htm
Awards: Coretta Scott King; Newbery
Subjects: contemporary issues; twentieth century

Questions

1. In which book does a character attack a wasp's nest in an old shed, believing it's a vampire bat?

2. In which book are two characters fed and sheltered in a homeless camp called Hooverville?

3. In which book does an old suitcase contain the few belongings a character has saved after his mother's death?

4. In which book is a character convinced that the bandleader whose picture is shown on a set of old flyers really is his father?

5. In which book does a rock collection help a character prove his identity?

Building Blocks

Cynthia Voigt. Scholastic, 1994. ISBN 0-590-47732-3 (pb).
URL: www.acs.ucalgary.ca/~dkbrown/k6/voigt.html
www.scils.rutgers.edu/special/kay/voigt.html
Subjects: fantasy; time travel

Questions

1. In which book does a character find himself living in the past, at the time when his father was a boy?

2. In which book does a character rescue someone from a cave?

3. In which book does a character discover his friend is also his contemporary father?

4. In which book does a character fall asleep in a basement fort and wake up in a similar fort in someone's bedroom?

5. In which book does a set of blocks made long ago for a father prove to have special powers?

Caddie Woodlawn

Carol Ryrie Brink. Macmillan, 1973, 1935. ISBN 0-02-713670-1 (hc);
ISBN 0-689-82969-8 (pb).
URL: www.connectingstudents.com/literacy/caddie.htm
www.sdcoe.k12.ca.us/score/caddie/caddietg.html
Awards: Newbery

Study Guides: LL; Portals; Lit. U.; Novel Units; LEAP; RBB; Sch.
Subjects: historical fiction; strong female

Questions

1. In which book does a family choose between remaining on the American frontier or returning to England when their father is offered the opportunity to become a wealthy aristocrat?

2. In which book does a character ride off to warn her Indian friends that there is talk of a massacre against them?

3. In which book is a character given a scalp belt by a friend?

4. In which book do children give a show, charging birds' nests and marbles for admission?

5. In which book is a character encouraged to run freely with her brothers, so she will grow up to be healthy?

Call It Courage

Armstrong Sperry. Simon & Schuster, 1968. ISBN 0-02-786030-2 (hc); ISBN 0-590-09063-1 (pb).
URL: www3.sympatico.ca/alanbrown/kids.htm
Awards: Newbery
Study Guides: LL; Portals; Lit. U.; Novel Units; LIFT
Subjects: adventure

Questions

1. In which book is Stout Heart the name of a coward?

2. In which book is there an albatross named Kivi and a dog named Uri?

3. In which book does a character make a knife and an axe out of whale bones?

4. In which book does a character save his dog from a hammerhead shark?

5. In which book does a character find that he is not a coward after all?

The Call of the Wild

Jack London. Atheneum, 1999. ISBN 0-689-1836-X.
URL: http://sunsite.berkeley.edu/London/
Study Guides: Lit. U.; Novel Units
Subjects: adventure; animals

Questions

1. In which book is a shepherd/St. Bernard mixed-breed sold to some shady characters on the Seattle docks?

2. In which book does a pampered animal from California learn to fight and steal food in order to survive in the Alaskan wilderness?

3. In which book does a dog named Buck serve as lead dog for a mail sled in Alaska?

4. In which book is an animal rescued from a fatal beating by John Thornton?

5. In which book does an animal pull a sled weighing 1,000 pounds?

The Castle in the Attic

Elizabeth Winthrop. Holiday, 1985. ISBN 0-8234-05789-6 (hc); ISBN 0-440-40941-1(pb).
URL: www.absolute-sway.com/winthrop/castleindex.html
Study Guides: Portals; Novel Units
Subjects: fantasy; time travel

Questions

1. In which book does William Edward Lawrence meet Sir Simon of Hargrave?

2. In which book does a character perform his gymnastics routine so a wicked wizard will hire him as a fool?

3. In which book does a character use a magic token to shrink a special friend?

4. In which book do characters fight a final battle against Alastor?

5. In which book does William become small in order to rescue a friend?

The Cat Who Went to Heaven

Elizabeth Coatsworth. Macmillan, 1990. ISBN 0-02-719710-7 (hc); ISBN 0-689-71433-5 (pb).
URL: www.powells.com/biblio/400-600/0027197107.html
Subjects: folklore

Questions

1. In which book does a picture of various animals visiting the Buddha fail to include the main character?

2. In which book does a Japanese housekeeper use food money to buy an animal?

3. In which book does an artist keep a tri-colored creature because such animals are thought to bring good luck?

4. In which book does a priest ask an artist to paint a picture of the death of Lord Buddha?

5. In which book is Good Fortune unhappy about being left out of a painting?

Catherine, Called Birdy

Karen Cushman. HarperCollins, 1994. ISBN 0-06-440-5842-2.
URL: www.ipl.org/youth/AskAuthor/cushmanbio.html
    www.carolhurst.com/titles/catherinecalledbirdy.html
Awards: Newbery
Study Guides: LL; Sch.
Subjects: historical fiction

Questions

1. In which book is the father of a thirteen-year-old determined to marry her off?

2. In which book does a character set fire to the manor privy to get rid of an unwanted suitor?

3. In which book does a character prefer running off to the Crusades to learning "ladylessons"?

4. In which book does a character try everything she can think of to avoid marrying the man she calls "Shaggy Beard"?

5. In which book is an abbess persuaded to add a dancing bear to her menagerie?

The Cay

Theodore Taylor. Doubleday, 1969. ISBN 0-385-07906-0 (hc); ISBN 0-380-00124-X (pb).
URL: www.eduplace.com/tview/tviews/khan70.html
Study Guides: LL; Sch.
Subjects: contemporary issues; survival

Questions

1. In which book do an old man, a boy, and a cat survive a shipwreck?

2. In which book does a character climb a coconut tree?

3. In which book are days counted by pebbles dropped into a can?

4. In which book does a character wonder if he will ever be able to see again?

5. In which book does an old man die in a tropical storm?

Charley Skedaddle

Patricia Beatty. William Morrow, 1987. ISBN 0-8167-1317-0 (pb)
URL: www.carolhurst.com/titles/charleysked.html
Study Guides: LL
Subjects: historical fiction—Civil War

Questions

1. In which book are two city gangs called the Bowery Boys and the Dead Skunks?

2. In which book does a twelve-year-old try to enlist in the Army?

3. In which book does a character learn that fighting in a war is an ugly and frightening experience?

4. In which book is a character locked in the hen house by an old mountain woman?

5. In which book does a character kill a panther using an old-fashioned long rifle?

Charlie and the Chocolate Factory

Roald Dahl. Random House, 1964. ISBN 0-394-71011-7 (hc); ISBN 0-553-15454-0 (pb).
URL: www.roalddahl.com/index2.htm
    www.connectingstudents.com/literacy/charlie.htm
Study Guides: LL; Portals; Lit. U.); Novel Units; LEAP
Subjects: fantasy

Questions

1. In which book is a character named Violet turned into a giant blueberry?

2. In which book does a character spend his remaining money on a winning candy bar?

3. In which book does a grandfather accompany a character on a prize trip through a manufacturing plant?

4. In which book are the Oompaloompas crazy about cacao beans?

5. In which book does a character win a golden ticket for a special trip?

Chasing Redbird

Sharon Creech. HarperCollins, 1997. ISBN 0-06-025987-1.
URL: www.sharoncreech.com/redbird.htm
    www.achuka.co.uk/scfile.htm
Subjects: family

Questions

1. In which book does a character find an old trail and decide to spend her summer clearing it?

2. In which book does a character steal a dog, a car, and his mother's ring to get attention?

3. In which book is a character sure that a boy is only being nice to her so that he can date her big sister, May?

4. In which book does a character learn to appreciate her own family after spending time camping out on her own?

5. In which book does a character find mementos of dead Cousin Rose in an old cabin hidden in the woods?

Children of the River

Linda Crew. Delacorte, 1989. ISBN 0-385-29690-8.
URL: www.jps.net/gmreed/lit/critic1.htm
    www.randomhouse.com/catalog/display.pperl?isbn=0440210224
Study Guides: LL; Novel Units; LIFT
Subjects: immigrants; prejudice

Questions

1. In which book does a character leave her family behind in Cambodia when the Khmer Rouge take over?

2. In which book does the high school football star become interested in a girl whose family are crop pickers?

3. In which book does the main character's aunt try to keep her from going out with the doctor's son?

4. In which book does a character learn that her old boyfriend has been killed by the Khmer Rouge?

5. In which book does the high school football champ quit the team because he doesn't like football?

The City of Gold and Lead

John Christopher. Macmillan, 1988. ISBN 0-02-04270-18.
URL: www.gnelson.demon.co.uk/Tripods.html
Subjects: science fiction

Questions

1. In which book is the world enslaved by giant three-legged Tripods from outer space?

2. In which book are adolescents fitted with caps to make them willing slaves to the Masters?

3. In which book do athletes compete for the honor of becoming slaves?

4. In which book does a character get into a tavern brawl and miss the boat going up the river?

5. In which book does a character learn of a plan to make the earth's atmosphere poisonous to humans?

Countdown

Ben Mikaelson. Hyperion, 1996. ISBN 0-7868-0252-9.
URL: www.benmikaelsen.com/books_countdown.htm
Subjects: adventure; other lands

Questions

1. In which book does a Maasai herder become part of a space shuttle mission?

2. In which book do characters from Kenya and Montana discover they have several things in common?

3. In which book is a character unable to go to the wood school because his father can't afford three cows for tuition?

4. In which book does a character cheat on a test and then confess to the instructors?

5. In which book is a character insistent on beating a girl in everything?

Crazy Lady

Jane Conly. HarperCollins, 1992. ISBN 0-06-021360-4 (hc); ISBN 0-06-440-5710 (pb).
URL: www.carr.org/authco/conly.htm
        www.childrensbookguild.org/conly.html
Awards: Newbery
Subjects: contemporary issues

Questions

1. In which book do characters tease an oddly dressed woman and her son?

2. In which book does an elderly retired teacher tutor a boy and encourage him to help her next door neighbors?

3. In which book does a widowed father sit up at night listening to old-time songs on the radio?

4. In which book does a character participate in the Special Olympics?

5. In which book does a mother send her only son to live with her sister because she is unable to break her drinking habit?

Danger in Quicksand Swamp

Bill Wallace. Pocket Books, 1991. ISBN 0-671-70898-8 (pb).
URL: http://title3.sde.state.ok.us/literatureanda/bill.htm
    www.pattonville.k12.mo.us/schools/roseacres/projects/readusa/ok.html
Subjects: adventure

Questions

1. In which book do two characters find a canoe buried in the sand?

2. In which book are some people marooned on an island surrounded by alligators?

3. In which book does a character use blue jeans and a belt to save another's life?

4. In which book do two characters trap a murderer in thick, loose sand?

5. In which book does a girl use a cork doll and treasure map to save their owner's life?

Danny, the Champion of the World

Roald Dahl. Penguin Putnam, 1999. ISBN 0-14130114-7 (pb).
URL: www.roalddahl.com/index2.htm
    www.puffin.co.uk/living/aut_59.html
Study Guides: LL; Sch.
Subjects: humor; families

Questions

1. In which book does a character live with his father in an old gypsy caravan behind a filling station?

2. In which book does a character help his father hunt illegally for pheasants?

3. In which book are plump raisins used to make the "horsehair stopper" and the "sticky hat"?

4. In which book are drunken birds hidden in a baby carriage?

5. In which book does a nine-year-old character set out in the middle of the night to find his father?

The Dark Is Rising

Susan Cooper. Margaret McElderry, 1973. ISBN 0-689-30317-3 (hc); ISBN 0-689-71087-9 (pb).
URL: www.puffin.co.uk/living/aut_10.html
    www.greenmanreview.com/dark_is_rising.html
Awards: Newbery
Study Guides: LL
Subjects: fantasy

Questions

1. In which book does a character learn on his eleventh birthday that he is the last of the Old Ones, born to receive the gift of power?

2. In which book is a character expected to find and guard the six great signs of the Powers of Light?

3. In which book is a character given an old book written in a strange language that tells ancient secrets?

4. In which book does a character sing Good King Wenceslas in both his own time and in a bygone day?

5. In which book does the burial ship of a medieval king rise out of the sea during a severe winter storm?

The Dark-thirty: Southern Tales of the Supernatural

Patricia McKissack. Random House, 1996. ISBN 0-679-91863-9 (hc).
URL: www.childrenslit.com/f_mckissack.html
        http://teacher.scholastic.com/authorsandbooks/authors/mckiss/bio.htm
Awards: Coretta Scott King, Newbery
Subjects: folklore

Questions

1. In which book does a character decide to live with a Sasquatch family?

2. In which book does someone visit a "conjure woman" to ask for a new baby brother?

3. In which book does a slave family turn into birds and fly away to freedom?

4. In which book does a woman with a sick baby haunt a bus route every winter?

5. In which book does a character believe a monster lives in the grandparents' chicken coop?

Dealing with Dragons

Patricia Wrede. Harcourt, 1990. ISBN 0-15-222900-0 (hc); ISBN 0-590-45722-5 (pb).
URL: www.dendarii.demon.co.uk/Wrede/
Subjects: fantasy

Questions

1. In which book does a princess volunteer to work for a dragon?

2. In which book is a princess tired of attempted rescues by knights and princes?

3. In which book does a princess talk a jinn into returning to his bottle for another 83 years?

4. In which book does a princess find knowledge of Latin and the ability to make cherries jubilee very useful skills?

5. In which book do two characters find that wizards melt in soap and water?

Dear Mr. Henshaw

Beverly Cleary. William Morrow, 1983. ISBN 0-688-02406-8 (hc); ISBN 0-440-41794-5 (pb).
URL: www.teleport.com/~krp/cleary.html
        www.trelease-on-reading.com/cleary.html
Awards: Newbery
Study Guides: Portals; Lit. U.; Novel Units; LIFT; RBB
Subjects: contemporary issues

Questions

1. In which book is the story told through letters written by a character to an author?

2. In which book does a character miss his truck driver father?

3. In which book does a character write about a book called "Ways to Amuse a Dog?"

4. In which book does a character invent a burglar alarm for his lunch box?

5. In which book is a character asked to answer 10 personal questions?

Diary of a Young Girl

Anne Frank. Bantam, 1993. ISBN 0-553-29698-1.
URL: www.annefrank.com/
     www-th.phys.rug.nl/~ma/annefrank.html
Study Guides: Scholastic
Subjects: classic; historical fiction—World War II; twentieth century

Questions

1. In which book does a character write down thoughts in a diary called "Kitty"?

2. In which book does a family have to be extremely quiet in the daytime so no one will hear them?

3. In which book does a family share their tiny apartment with a dentist and another family?

4. In which book does a hungry family find one of their guests stealing food?

5. In which book does a character manage to make Hanukkah presents for everyone out of scraps?

Dicey's Song

Cynthia Voigt. Atheneum, 1982. ISBN 0-689-30944-9 (hc); ISBN 0-449-70276-6 (pb).
URL: www.acs.ucalgary.ca/~dkbrown/k6/voigt.html
     www.scils.rutgers.edu/special/kay/voigt.html
Awards: Newbery
Study Guides: LL; Portals; Lit. U.; Novel Units
Subjects: contemporary issues; families

Questions

1. In which book does a character clean a store to get allowance money for her brothers and sisters?

2. In which book does a character get into a fight when he is teased about his grandmother?

3. In which book do the main characters plan ways to help Maybelle learn?

4. In which book is a character's composition used by the teacher as an example of plagiarism?

5. In which book do two girls discuss the best way of choosing friends?

The Dollhouse Murders

Betty Ren Wright. Holiday, 1983. ISBN 0-8234-0497-8 (hc); ISBN 0-590-43461-6 (pb)

URL: http://library.thinkquest.org/J001776/wright.html
www.maquoketa.k12.ia.us/87_88letter.html
Subjects: mystery

Questions

1. In which book does a character fall in love with an old object hidden in an attic?

2. In which book does a character discover the secret of her grandparents' unexplained death?

3. In which book does an aunt admit to suspicion that her fiancé killed her parents?

4. In which book is the answer to an old murder found in a letter hidden in a book?

5. In which book is a special toy belonging to her aunt given as a present to a character?

The Door in the Wall

Marguerite DeAngeli. Doubleday, 1989. ISBN 0-385-07283-X (hc); ISBN 0-440-91164-8 (pb).
URL: www.lapeer.lib.mi.us/Library/Exhibits/MdA/index.html
Awards: Newbery
Subjects: historical fiction—Middle Ages

Questions

1. In which book does a character on crutches escape from a castle, climb down a ravine, and swim across two rivers?

2. In which book does a character learn to use woodcarving tools?

3. In which book is a character nicknamed "Crookshanks"?

4. In which book does a knight rescue a character who is crippled?

5. In which book is a character deserted by his servants?

A Door Near Here

Heather Quarles. Delacorte, 1998. ISBN 0-385-32595-9 (hc); ISBN 0-440-22761-5 (pb).
URL: www.cslewis.drzeus.net/
www.powells.com/biblio/29000-29200/0385325959.html
Notes: Mature theme
Subjects: contemporary issues; families

Questions

1. In which book is an eight-year-old hidden under the bleachers in a high school gym?

2. In which book does a character write a letter to C. S. Lewis asking for directions to Narnia?

3. In which book is a tree house used for a family meeting place?

4. In which book is the electricity turned off because an alcoholic mother has not paid the bill?

5. In which book do three teenagers go grocery shopping in the middle of the night?

Dragon's Gate

Laurence Yep. HarperCollins, 1993. ISBN 0-06-022971-3.
URL: www.scils.rutgers.edu/special/kay/yep.html
Awards: Newbery
Study Guides: Lit. U.; Connect
Subjects: historical fiction

Questions

1. In which book does a character dream of joining his father and uncle in "The Land of the Golden Mountain"?

2. In which book does Otter discover that his father is a railroad worker instead of a rich influential man?

3. In which book does a character climb the snow-covered Tiger mountain in order to set off an avalanche?

4. In which book do two outcasts—a Chinese and an American—become friends in spite of their fathers?

5. In which book does a character persuade his fellow workers to strike so they can improve their wages and living conditions?

Dragon's Milk

Susan Fletcher. Aladdin, 1996. ISBN 0-689-71623-0.
Subjects: fantasy

Questions

1. In which book does a character see the future in her clay?

2. In which book are Pyro, Embyr and Synge important characters?

3. In which book does a grandmother tell a character to leave home dressed as a boy and to follow a kestrel?

4. In which book do baby animals rise, flame, and fall in their sleep?

5. In which book does a character discover she is a Krag by birth, not an Elythian?

Dragonsong

Anne McCaffrey. Atheneum, 1976. ISBN 0-553-54176-5 (pb).
URL: www.annemccaffrey.org
      www.randomhouse.com/delrey/pern/amcc/
Subjects: fantasy

Questions

1. In which book is a character forbidden to become a harper because she is a girl?

2. In which book do harpers teach history by means of ballads?

3. In which book does a character find and impress baby fire lizards?

4. In which book do people use dragons to fly "between time"?

5. In which book does burning thread periodically fall from the sky?

The Ear, the Eye, and the Arm

Nancy Farmer. Orchard Books, 1994. ISBN 0-531-08679-8 (hc).
URL: www.powells.com/biblio/11000-11200/0140376410.html
Awards: Newbery
Notes: Mature theme
Study Guides: LIFT
Subjects: science fiction

Questions

1. In which book does a family have robot servants, artificial bird songs, and an automated watchdog?

2. In which book does a large group of people make their home in a neighborhood known as the Cow's Guts?

3. In which book are three children kidnapped and forced to dig up trash in an underground tunnel?

4. In which book are twentieth-century characters held captive in a village that existed long ago?

5. In which book do some characters whose mother drank contaminated water display unusual characteristics from birth?

Earthshine

Theresa Nelson. Laurel Leaf, 1996. ISBN 0-440-21989-2 (pb).
URL: www.powells.com/biblio/36400-36600/0440219892.html
Subjects: contemporary issues

Questions

1. In which book is a girl's father dying of AIDS?

2. In which book does an article in an old newspaper lead a character to believe in miracle cures for illness?

3. In which book does a character take a clock apart to make it stop ticking?

4. In which book is a carnival broken up by a carload of skinheads wearing swastikas?

5. In which book does a field of wildflowers seem like a miracle to a busload of travelers?

Ella Enchanted

Gail Levine. Scholastic, 1998. ISBN 0-590-64608-7 (pb).
URL: www.alexlibris.com/bio_carsonlevine.asp
     www.edupaperback.org/authorbios/Levine_GailCarson.html
Awards: Newbery
Subjects: fantasy

Questions

1. In which book does a girl always have to obey orders?

2. In which book is the family cook really a fairy godmother?

3. In which book is a fairy changed into a squirrel to learn the dangers in giving gifts?

4. In which book does a girl break the curse laid on her when she refuses to marry the man she loves because she knows her curse will be dangerous to him?

5. In which book does a magic book show a girl what her friends are doing while she is away at school?

The Empress of Elsewhere

Theresa Nelson. Dorling Kindersley, 1998. ISBN 0-7894-2498-3 (hc).
URL: www.eyeontomorrow.com/embracingthechild/anelson.htm
Subjects: contemporary issues

Questions

1. In which book do some characters rescue a runaway monkey?

2. In which book does a character wear a wolf-head cap and bite people who come to see her?

3. In which book do three children rebuild an old tree house on a private island?

4. In which book do some characters smuggle an animal onto a bus and travel to the Houston zoo?

5. In which book does a character believe she caused her father's death in an accident by drinking too much iced tea?

The Endless Steppe

Esther Hautzig. Harper, 1968. ISBN 0-06-440577-X (pb).
URL: www.powells.com/biblio/6000-6200/006440577X.html
Study Guides: LL; LIFT
Subjects: historical fiction—World War II

Questions

1. In which book is a Polish family deported to Siberia to work in a gypsum mine?

2. In which book does a character cut off her long hair in order to be accepted by the other children in her new school?

3. In which book is the author telling about her own childhood experiences in Eastern Europe?

4. In which book does a character use yarn from an old skirt to knit a new sweater?

5. In which book are the mother and grandmother forced to work with dynamite?

The Face on the Milk Carton

Caroline B. Cooney. Bantam Doubleday Dell, 1994. ISBN 0-440-22065-3.
URL: www.scils.rutgers.edu/special/kay/cooney5.html
Study Guides: Novel Units
Subjects: contemporary issues; mystery

Questions

1. In which book does a character want to change the spelling of her plain name?

2. In which book do childhood pictures on a stairway wall give a clue to a character's adoption?

3. In which book does an 800 number seem both frightening and enticing?

4. In which book do some characters play hooky in order to find out the truth?

5. In which book is a character faced with decisions regarding two families who love her?

The Fellowship of the Ring

J.R.R. Tolkien. Houghton Mifflin, 1988. ISBN 0-395-4893-18.
URL: www.csclub.uwaterloo.ca/u/relipper/tolkien/rootpage.html
Subjects: fantasy

Questions

1. In which book do Sam Gamgee and Pippin insist on accompanying Frodo on a journey?

2. In which book is a ranger called Strider really named Aragorn?

3. In which book do Eleven doors open for the company of Nine?

4. In which book are people who hate being above ground required to spend a night up in the trees on a wooden platform?

5. In which book is the power of Sauron taking over the land?

The Fighting Ground

Avi. Harper, 1987. ISBN 0-064-44018-5.
URL: www.avi-writer.com/
    www.carr.org/read/fiction.htm
Study Guides: LL
Subjects: historical fiction

Questions

1. In which book does a character borrow a gun that is taller than he is?

2. In which book does the hero have to choose between carrying a child and a gun?

3. In which book does a character try to protect his enemies because they were kind to him?

4. In which book are neighbors killed because they are siding with the English?

5. In which book do we follow a character for one day as he sees his friends wounded, buries people he doesn't know, and becomes a prisoner?

Fire on the Wind

Linda Crew. Delacorte, 1995. ISBN 0-385-32185-6.
URL: www.randomhouse.com/teachers/authors/crew.html
Subjects: historical fiction; twentieth century

Questions

1. In which book does a mother owl bring rodents to her rescued baby?

2. In which book does a character name a fawn Snowflake?

3. In which book are family homes mounted on skids, so the train can carry them wherever the logging company needs them?

4. In which book does a father want the main character to work in a cook camp instead of going to school?

5. In which book does a character race down railroad tracks to rescue some loggers?

The Fledgling

Jane Langton. Harper, 1980. ISBN 0-06-023679-5 (hc); ISBN 0-06-440121-9 (pb).
URL: www.hymnfortheproducts.com/hner/0064401219
Subjects: fantasy

Questions

1. In which book is a character using a magic feather really able to fly?

2. In which book does Madeline believe that the main character is from fairyland and not a real girl?

3. In which book is a character shot when mistaken for a goose?

4. In which book does a character live near Walden Pond?

5. In which book is a character given a blue and white ball that becomes the mirror of the earth?

Forged by Fire

Sharon M. Draper. Atheneum, 1997. ISBN 0-689-80699-X.
URL: www.sharondraper.com/
Awards: Coretta Scott King
Subjects: contemporary issues

Questions

1. In which book does a three-year-old start a fire by playing with his mother's cigarette lighter?

2. In which book does an aunt take in her nephew when his mother goes to jail?

3. In which book does a character use an old wheelchair to make a go-cart?

4. In which book does Angel win a prize for her dancing?

5. In which book does a character try to keep his little sister safe from his stepfather's abuse?

Frindle

Andrew Clements. Simon & Schuster, 1996. ISBN 0-689-80669-8 (hc); ISBN 0-689-81876-9 (pb).
URL: www.edupaperback.org/authorbios/Clements_Andrew.html
        www.emporia.edu/libsv/press99.htm
Subjects: contemporary issues; school stories

Questions

1. In which book does a character ask many questions to distract his teachers from giving homework assignments?

2. In which book does a character find he cannot stop a prank once it's started?

3. In which book do a character and friends find themselves on "Good Morning, America" and "The Late Show"?

4. In which book did a character take a dictionary lesson to heart?

5. In which book is a woman known as the "Lone Granger" surprised when a scholarship is set up in her name?

The Frog Princess of Pelham

Ellen Conford. Little Brown, 1997. ISBN 0-316 152463.
URL: www.twbookmark.com/books/91/0316152463/index.html
Subjects: humor

Questions

1. In which book does a character have to go to a Survival Camp in Idaho for her summer vacation?

2. In which book does an animal trash a room while trying to get a little exercise?

3. In which book do the CIA and National Institute of Science search a house in the name of national security?

4. In which book does anger cause the main character to swell up like a balloon?

5. In which book is a kiss the "beginning" of a friendship?

From the Mixed-up Files of Mrs. Basil E. Frankweiler

E.L. Konigsburg. Atheneum, 1970. ISBN 0-440-91107-9 (pb).
URL: www.randomhouse.com/teachers/authors/koni.html
    www3.sympatico.ca/alanbrown/kids.htm
Awards: Newbery
Study Guides: LL; Portals; Lit. U.; Novel Units; LIFT; RBB; Sch.
Subjects: contemporary issues; strong female

Questions

1. In which book do some characters solve a mystery about a statue they call "Angel"?

2. In which book do two siblings collect money from a fountain during the night so they can buy food during the day?

3. In which book does a character run away from home because she thinks it will teach her family a lesson in "Claudia Appreciation"?

4. In which book do the characters find that a favorite statue was carved by the greatest sculptor of all—Michaelangelo?

5. In which book do two characters hide out in an art museum?

Frozen Summer

Mary Jane Auch. Holt, 1998. ISBN 0-8050-4923-1 (hc).
URL: http://members.nbci.com/maryjaneauch/
    www.powells.com/biblio/94600-94800/0805049231.html
Subjects: historical fiction—pioneer life; strong female

Questions

1. In which book does a character accidentally put out the cabin fire as she tries to assist in a baby's birth?

2. In which book does a father forbid a character to invite her grandmother to visit?

3. In which book do some wilderness settlers believe that a crop-killing cold spell means that the end of the world is coming?

4. In which book does a character sweep a tavern floor to earn money for a cup of tea?

5. In which book does a character learn to snare rabbits and tickle trout to get food for the family?

A Gathering of Days

Joan Blos. Scribner's , 1979. ISBN 0-684-16340-3 (hc); ISBN 0-689-82291-4 (pb).
URL: http://falcon.jmu.edu/~ramseyil/blos.htm
Awards: Newbery
Study Guides: LL
Subjects: historical fiction

Questions

1. Which book is presented as the diary of thirteen-year-old girl?

2. In which book does a gift of a piece of lace tell a character that a runaway slave is now free?

3. In which book does a new stepmother teacher a character how to quilt?

4. In which book is a journal written during the years 1830-32?

5. In which book is the setting the state of New Hampshire some years before the Civil War?

Gentle Ben

Walt Morey. Puffin 1992. ISBN 0-1403035-2 (pb).
URL: www.pcez.com/~hobbit/morey.htm
Study Guides: Novel Units
Subjects: Alaska; animals

Questions

1. In which book is a chained bear attacked by men with a scythe?

2. In which book does an animal save a family from fish pirates?

3. In which book are Fog Benson and Mud Hole Jones important characters?

4. In which book does a character have an Alaskan brown bear as a pet?

5. In which book does a family hide an animal from a determined hunter?

The Gentleman Outlaw and Me—Eli

Mary Downing Hahn. Clarion, 1996. ISBN 0-395-73083-X (hc).
URL: www.childrensbookguild.org/hahn.html
    www.carr.org/authco/hahn.htm
Subjects: historical fiction; strong female

Questions

1. In which book does a character travel west with her dog, Caesar?

2. In which book does a girl take overalls from a clothesline to disguise herself as a boy?

3.   In which book does a young man from the east try to become a western gunman?

4. In which book do two travelers trick gamblers in small town saloons to win money for their journey?

5. In which book does a sheriff learn that one of two arrested horse thieves is his daughter?

Ghost Canoe

Will Hobbs. William Morrow, 1997. ISBN 0-688-14 193-5 (hc); ISBN 0-380-72537- 1 (pb)
URL: www.randomhouse.com/teachers/guides/drrt.html
Subjects: historical fiction

Questions

1. In which book does an old letter help solve a murder and a robbery?

2. In which book does a character do magic tricks to get the natives to accept him?

3. In which book does a character go on a whale hunt in a canoe?

4. In which book is a map secreted inside some bone "sla hal" game pieces?

5. In which book is a merchant's money stolen to be used to buy a trading post?

A Ghost in the Family

Betty Ren Wright. Scholastic, 1998. ISBN 0-590-02955-X.
URL: www.powells.com/biblio/56000-56200/059002955X.html
Subjects: mystery

Questions

1. In which book does a character stay in a room inhabited by the spirit of a dead dentist?

2. In which book does a character's view into the window of a neighbor's room help to solve a mystery?

3. In which book does the message "Go Home" appear on a bathroom mirror?

4. In which book do the characters solve the mystery of a missing diamond bracelet?

5. In which book do you read about a flying toothbrush, snakes in the closet, and humongous beetles on the bed?

The Ghost of Fossil Glen

Cynthia DeFelice. Farrar, Straus and Giroux, 1998. ISBN 0-374-31787-9 (hc); ISBN 0-380-73175-4 (pb).
URL: www.libsci.sc.edu/scasl/ghost.htm
   www.maquoketa.k12.ia.us/defelice.html
Subjects: contemporary issues

Questions

1. In which book does a mysterious voice help a character climb down from a dangerous cliff?

2. In which book does a character receive the unexplained gift of a diary in her mailbox?

3. In which book do a character's friends watch a TV show called, "Teen Twins"?

4. In which book does a golden retriever help solve a four-year-old mystery?

5. In which book are the natural wonders of a canyon saved from development as a subdivision?

Gib Rides Home

Zilpha Keatley Snyder. Bantam Doubleday Dell, 1998. ISBN 0-440-41257-9 .
URL: www.microweb.com/lsnyder
   www3.sympatico.ca/alanbrown/kids.htm
Subjects: families; historical fiction—twentieth century

Questions

1. In which book does a character hide in a horse's stall after running away from an abusive farmer?

2. In which book does a "farmed out" orphan recognize an old man and a pair of horses from his childhood?

3. In which book does a ranch hand's broken leg help a character find a home?

4. In which book does a character who hates horses learn to ride a high-spirited mare?

5. In which book is someone's first automobile ride an unhappy occasion?

A Girl Called Boy

Belinda Hurmence. Ticknor Fields, 1982. ISBN 0-395-55698-8 (pb).
URL: www.sunsite.utk.edu/civil-war/
Subjects: historical fiction—Civil War

Questions

1. In which book does a character become bored by tales of her family's past as slaves?

2. In which book does a father carry an old soapstone luck charm that he calls "the Freedom Bird"?

3. In which book does a character find herself in a slave family when she travels back in time to the year 1853?

4. In which book do pants make a girl appear to be a boy in the days of her great-grandparents?

5. In which book does a character teach friends how to write, even though it is against the law?

A Girl from Yamhill

Beverly Cleary. William Morrow, 1988. ISBN 0-688-07800-1.
URL: www.teleport.com/~krp/cleary.html
     http://falcon.jmu.edu/~ramseyil/cleary.htm
Subjects: biography

Questions

1. In which book does a character receive lots of love from Grandma and Grandpa Atlee?

2. In which book does a mother start a county library because her daughter asks for stories so often?

3. In which book does a character win $2.00 from a writing contest because no one else entered?

4. In which book does a group earn a free week at Campfire camp by visiting four factories in one day?

5. In which book does the Great Depression cause a father to lose his job at the bank?

A Girl Named Disaster

Nancy Farmer. Orchard, 1996. ISBN 0-531-08889-8 (hc); ISBN 0-14-038635-1 (pb).
URL: www.powells.com/cgi-bin/biblio?inkey=7-0140386351-0
Awards: Newbery
Subjects: contemporary issues; survival

Questions

1. In which book has a character's mother been killed by a leopard?

2. In which book does a grandmother encourage her granddaughter to steal a boat and run away from her village?

3. In which book does cholera kill many people?

4. In which book does a character live for many weeks with a tribe of baboons?

5. In which book does a character mistake a magazine ad for a picture of her mother?

The Giver

Lois Lowry. Bantam Doubleday Dell, 1993. ISBN 0-440-21907-8.
URL: www.scils.rutgers.edu/special/kay/lowry.html
     www.carolhurst.com/authors/llowry.html
Awards: Newbery

Study Guides: Portals; Lit. U.; Novel Units; LIFT; Sch.

Subjects: fantasy

Questions

1. In which book are the highest personal qualities (intelligence, integrity, courage, wisdom, and the capacity to see beyond) required before you can become the Receiver?

2. In which book did doing away with differences mean there was no color or sunshine in the characters' world?

3. In which book does the statement "being released" mean being put to death?

4. In which book does a family dinner ritual include discussing experiences and feelings and how the rules of the community apply to them?

5. In which book do children wear jackets that button in the back so that they will learn to help one another?

The Golden Compass

Philip Pullman. Ballantine, 1995. ISBN 0-345-41335-8.

URL: www.puffin.co.uk/living/aut_41.html
      www.randomhouse.com/features/pullman/index.html.

Subjects: fantasy

Questions

1. In which book do armor-wearing bears hold a father captive?

2. In which book does a character rescue Iorek Byrnison by finding out where his armor is hidden?

3. In which book is a character brought up by scholars in an Oxford College?

4. In which book does a character learn about using an alethiometer—an instrument for revealing truthful answers?

5. In which book are children kidnapped by the Gobblers?

The Great Gilly Hopkins

Katherine Paterson. Harper & Row, 1987. ISBN 0-590-61389-8 (pb).

URL: www.ipl.org/youth/AskAuthor/paterson.html

Awards: Newbery

Study Guides: LL; Portals; Novel Units; LIFT; Sch.

Subjects: comtemporary issues; strong female

Questions

1. In which book has a character lived in three foster families in the last three years?

2. In which book does a girl fight six boys on her first day in a new school?

3. In which book does a character steal money from a blind neighbor?

4. In which book does a tough girl give survival training to a boy who wears glasses?

5. In which book does a character try to buy a ticket to go to San Francisco and end up in the police station?

The Great Wheel

Robert Lawson. Walker, 1993. ISBN 0-80277392-3.
URL: www.friend.ly.net/scoop/biographies/lawsonrobert/
Subjects: historical fiction

Questions

1. In which book does a boy write to a girlfriend even though he doesn't have her address?

2. In which book does someone create a ride capable of carrying more than 2,000 passengers per trip?

3. In which book does a neighbor read tea leaves in a cup and correctly predict the future?

4. In which book does a character's home come from a ride in an amusement park?

5. In which book do we learn about the Chicago Columbian Exposition?

The Grey King

Susan Cooper. Margaret McElderry Books, 1975. ISBN 0-689-50029-7 (hc); ISBN 0-689-82988-4 (pb).
URL: http://missy.shef.ac.uk/~emp94ms/mceld.html
        www.puffin.co.uk/living/aut_10.html
Awards: Newbery
Subjects: fantasy

Questions

1. In which book are six sleepers wakened by a golden harp to fight against the dark forces?

2. In which book does a character learn that he is the son of King Arthur?

3. In which book does a dog with silver eyes see the wind and the gales?

4. In which book does the last of the Old Ones appear to battle in service of the Light?

5. In which book does a girl learn that she is also Queen Guinevere?

Habibi

Naomi Shihab Nye. Simon & Schuster, 1997. ISBN 0-689-80149-1 (hc); ISBN 0-689-82323-4 (pb).
URL: http://arabia.com/article/0,1690,Life%7C29705,00.html
        www.ala.org/booklist/v94/youth/se2/57nye.html
Subjects: contemporary issues; other lands; strong female

Questions

1. In which book does a family move from St. Louis, Missouri, to a small community near Jerusalem?

2. In which book is a new student surprised to see the principal wearing a burgundy robe and a giant, pointed hat?

3. In which book do a boy and his sister meet new friends while they are chasing the hen that they let out of her coop?

4. In which book is the father dismayed when his daughter tells him that the boy of

her dreams is of a different religion?

5. In which book do children from several warring groups realize that they must be the ones to bring peace to their land?

Half Magic

Edward Eager. Harcourt, 1954, 1999. ISBN 0-15-202069-1 (hc); ISBN 0-15-202068-3 (pb).
URL: www.geocities.com/Athens/Delphi/1287/index.html
     http://teacher.scholastic.com/authorsandbooks/bestbooks/books4-8/halfmagic.htm
Subjects: contemporary fantasy

Questions

1. In which book does a character find a magic coin which makes wishes come partly true?

2. In which book does a boy wish to be on a desert island and find himself on a desert?

3. In which book does a cat half-talk and an iron dog come halfway to life?

4. In which book does a character from modern times fight and defeat Sir Lancelot in a tournament?

5. In which book does a magic charm cause a mother to feel that she has lost her mind?

Harriet the Spy

Louise Fitzhugh. HarperCollins, 1964. ISBN 0-06-021911-4 (hc); ISBN 0-06-440-660-1 (pb).
URL: www.familyeducation.com/article/0,1120,22-10814,00.html
     www.nancymatson.com/HTHESP.HTM
Awards: Newbery
Study Guides: Portals; Lit. U.; Novel Units
Subjects: school stories

Questions

1. In which book is a character angry when she is left out of a sixth grade club?

2. In which book does a character call her nanny "Ole Golly"?

3. In which book does a character carry a flashlight, notebook, pen, canteen, and Boy Scout knife on her tool belt?

4. In which book does a character wear a special costume and write down everything she sees her neighbors doing?

5. In which book does a character become editor of the sixth-grade page in the newspaper?

Harry Potter and the Chamber of Secrets

J. K. Rowling. Scholastic, 1999. ISBN 1-12151404-9.
URL: www.bloomsbury.com/harrypotter/
     www.scholastic.com/harrypotter/home.asp
Subjects: fantasy; school stories

Questions

1. In which book do some characters get into trouble as they try to get back to boarding school?

2. In which book does a character hear a mysterious voice in the walls that no one else can hear?

3. In which book do classmates suspect that a character is related to an evil wizard?

4. In which book does an old diary reveal the secret of a mysterious passage and a hidden reptile's den?

5. In which book does a character fall into the power of an evil wizard by writing in an old diary?

Harry Potter and the Sorcerer's Stone

J. K. Rowling. Scholastic, 1999. ISBN 0-590-35340-3 (hc); ISBN 0-590-35342-X (pb).
URL: www.trelease-on-reading.com/whatsnu_harryp.html
   www.mikids.com/harrypotter
Subjects: fantasy; school stories

Questions

1. In which book is a green-eyed baby with a lightning scar on his forehead left on a doorstep?

2. In which book does a character receive an avalanche of letters on his eleventh birthday?

3. In which book does a character learn quidditch, a game played on flying brooms?

4. In which book does a character receive a cloak of invisibility as a Christmas present?

5. In which book does a scar on his forehead both warn someone of evil and then provide protection from it?

The Haymeadow

Gary Paulsen. Dell, 1992. ISBN 0-440-40923-3.
URL: www.carolhurst.com/titles/haymeadow.html
   www.scils.rutgers.edu/special/kay/paulsen.html
Subjects: contemporary issues

Questions

1. In which book is a fourteen-year-old left alone for the summer to tend a herd of sheep?

2. In which book is a wagon washed into a creek by a flash flood?

3. In which book is a camp attacked by coyotes and a bear?

4. In which book does a character eat "surprise" meals after the labels on his canned foods are destroyed?

5. In which book does a character learn surprising truths about his much-admired great-grandfather?

Heaven

Angela Johnson. Simon & Schuster, 1998. ISBN 0-689-82229-4.
URL: www.powells.com/biblio/76600-76800/0689822294.html
Awards: Coretta Scott King
Subjects: families

Questions

1. In which book does a character treasure letters from her wandering Uncle Jake?

2. In which book does a character love babysitting Bobby's daughter Feather?

3. In which book is Shoogy totally unlike the rest of her family?

4. In which book does a character suddenly discover that the people she thinks of as her parents are really her uncle and aunt?

5. In which book does a family move to a small Ohio town because of a postcard, Western Union, and Uncle Jack?

The Hero and the Crown

Robin McKinley. Greenwillow, 1984. ISBN 0-688-02593-5 (hc); ISBN 0-441-00499-7 (pb).
URL: www.sff.net/people/robin-mckinley/
Awards: Newbery
Subjects: contemporary issues; fantasy

Questions

1. In which book does a character use a red jewel made of dragon blood to defeat her wicked uncle?

2. In which book does a character discover an ointment that protects against dragon fire?

3. Which book takes place in the imaginary land of Damar?

4. In which book does a princess defeat the Black Dragon?

5. In which book is a character the only member of her family who does not possess magic powers?

The High King

Lloyd Alexander. Holt, 1968, 1999. ISBN 0-8050-6135-5 (hc).
URL: www.carr.lib.md.us/authco/ale-high.htm
Awards: Newbery
Study Guides: LL
Subjects: fantasy

Questions

1. In which book does a character search for Gwydion's enchanted sword, which has been stolen?

2. In which book does the Lord of the Dead meet final defeat?

3. In which book are some characters freed by wolves?

4. In which book does a princess give up her enchanted powers for the sake of love?

5. In which book does an assistant pig keeper become Lord of the kingdom?

Hiroshima

Laurence Yep. Scholastic, 1995. ISBN : 00-590-20832-2.
URL: www.scils.rutgers.edu/special/kay/yep.html
Subjects: contemporary issues; historical fiction—World War II

Questions

1. Which book is the true story of an event ending the second World War?

2. In which book do some classmates work at tearing down houses in the city?

3. In which book does a girl go to New York City for surgery?

4. In which book does Riko hear about a bomber through her work at recording phone messages for the army?

5. In which book is there a statue of Sadako holding a golden crane over her head?

The Hobbit

J.R.R. Tolkien. Houghton Mifflin, 1938. ISBN 0-395-07122-4 (hc); ISBN 0-618-00221-9 (pb).
URL: www.tolkien.cro.net/index.html
Study Guides: Lit. U.; Novel Units
Subjects: fantasy, classic

Questions

1. In which book does a dragon menace some travelers?

2. In which book does a character live in a comfortable round hole in a hill?

3. In which book can a beekeeper change his skin to become a huge black bear?

4. In which book do two characters challenge each other to solve riddles?

5. In which book do some spiders web-wrap a group of dwarves for their dinner?

Holes

Louis Sachar. Farrar, Straus and Giroux, 1998. ISBN 0-374-33265-7.
URL: www.cbcbooks.org/navigation/autindex.htm
Awards: Newbery
Subjects: contemporary issues

Questions

1. In which book does a character undo his grandfather's curse when he carries a friend up a mountain?

2. In which book is there a bandit named Kissin' Kate Barlow?

3. In which book are the family problems based on the "no-good-dirty-rotten-pig-stealing-great-great-grandfather"?

4. In which book is Green Lake actually a vast dried-up desert in the middle of Texas?

5. In which book is the warden a descendant of a bandit who kissed the men she killed?

Homecoming

Cynthia Voigt. Atheneum, 1981. ISBN 0-689-30833-7 (hc); ISBN 449-70254-5 (pb).
URL: www.scils.rutgers.edu/special/kay/voigt.html
Study Guides: Portals; Novel Units; LIFT
Subjects: contemporary issues; families

Questions

1. In which book are some children left alone in a parked car in a shopping center?

2. In which book do some characters tell lies to help their family?

3. In which book do the children learn that their aunt has died and their cousin Eunice wants to send them to foster homes?

4. In which book does a character manage to take her brothers and sisters to their aunt's house, even though they have been left alone with almost no money?

5. In which book does a character wash windows in a gas station so she can get a map of Connecticut?

I Rode a Horse of Milk White Jade

Diane Lee Wilson. Orchard, 1998. ISBN 0-531-33024-9 (hc); ISBN 06-440173-X (pb).
URL: http://tlc.ai.org/wilsondl.htm
Subjects: animals; historical fiction; other lands; strong female

Questions

1. In which book does a grandmother tell an exciting story while waiting for a birth?

2. In which book is a character's mother killed by lightning?

3. In which book does a character select an old, lame mare when she might have chosen the horse of her dreams?

4. In which book does a character replace her cousin as soldiers are taking him away to serve in the army?

5. In which book does a character make a long, hazardous journey as an Arrow Rider for the emperor?

I'm Not Who You Think I Am

Peg Kehret. Dutton, 1999. ISBN 0-525-46153-1 (hc)
URL: www.pioneerdrama.com/playwrights/pk.html
Subjects: contemporary issues; mystery

Questions

1. In which book does a woman think she's found her long-lost daughter?

2. In which book do some very vocal parents try to get the basketball coach fired?

3. In which book does a character believe she might have been adopted because she's short, the rest of her family is tall, and her hair is a different color from theirs?

4. In which book do the words "Live with Purpose and Honor" on the poster tell a character what to do with her videos?

5. In which book does someone understand that her friend's signal of rubbing the left ear as a call for help?

The Incredible Journey

Sheila Burnford. Little Brown, 1961. ISBN 0-440-41324-9 (pb).
Study Guides: Portals; Lit. U.; Novel Units; LIFT
Subjects: animals; survival

Questions

1. In which book do a Siamese cat, a Labrador retriever, and an old Bull Terrier become traveling companions?

2. In which book does an Indian woman believe she has seen a good omen when a white dog gives meat to a cat?

3. In which book does a cat save an old dog from a mother bear and her cubs?

4. In which book does a cat escape from a lynx by hiding in a rabbit burrow?

5. In which book do two families realize that their lost animals are traveling a straight route west?

The Indian in the Cupboard

Lynne Reid Banks. Doubleday, 1985. ISBN 0-385-17051-3 (hc); ISBN 0-380-72558-4 (pb)
URL: www.inconnect.com/~renshaw/indiancupboard.html
Study Guides: LL; Portals; Lit. U.; Novel Units; LIFT; RBB; Sch.
Subjects: fantasy

Questions

1. In which book do plastic toys come to life when they are put in an old cabinet?

2. In which book does a character receive an old plastic toy for a birthday present?

3. In which book does a character learn to let his toys work out their own destiny?

4. In which book are some Indians allowed to return to their own time?

5. In which book do some characters care for a cowboy and an Iroquois Indian?

Invincible Louisa

Cornelia Meigs. Little Brown, 1933. ISBN 0-316-56594-6 (pb).
URL: www.alcottweb.com/
Awards: Newbery
Subjects: biography

Questions

1. Which book is a biography of the author of Little Women?

2. In which book does a child almost drown in the frog pond on Boston Commons?

3. In which book does a character get typhoid fever while nursing soldiers during the Civil War?

4. In which book is it predicted that an aspiring writer will never be successful?

5. In which book does a character find a slave hiding in a Dutch oven?

The Iron Ring

Lloyd Alexander. Dutton, 1997. ISBN 0-525-45597-3.
URL: www.cbcbooks.org/navigation/autindex.htm
Subjects: fantasy

Questions

1. In which book do ants build a house around a man while he sits meditating in the woods?

2. In which book does an eagle drop a precious stone into a lake when he opens his beak to answer a taunt?

3. In which book does a young king help an elephant to escape a cruel master and a tiger to get out of a pit?

4. In which book does an old man carry a white umbrella into battle?

5. In which book does a character explain a system called "The Choosing"?

Ishi, Last of His Tribe

Theodora Kroeber. Bantam, 1984. ISBN 0-553-24898-7.
URL: http://emuseum.mnsu.edu/information/biography/klmno/kroeberquinn_theodora.html
www.cateweb.org/
Subjects: historical fiction—Native American; survival

Questions

1. In which book does a sheriff find a wild man crouching by a fence?

2. In which book is "siwini" the first word a Yahi Indian and an anthropologist can recognize?

3. In which book do the white men manage to kill all the members of a tribe, except one?

4. In which book does an Indian mother tell her son that the train engine is a demon that follows white men wherever they go?

5. In which book does an Indian make his home in a museum?

Island of the Blue Dolphins

Scott O'Dell. Houghton Mifflin, 1960, 1997. ISBN 0-395-06962-9 (hc);
ISBN 0-440-91043-9 (pb).
URL: www.randomhouse.com/teachers/authors/odel.html
Awards: Newbery

Study Guides: Sch.
Subjects: historical fiction—Native American; survival

Questions

1. In which book are two youngsters left alone on an uninhabited island?

2. In which book does a wild dog become a solitary child's companion?

3. In which book is character killed by a pack of wild dogs?

4. In which book does a character watch for strangers from a bluff?

5. In which book does a character spend 18 years alone on an island?

Izzy, Willy Nilly

Cynthia Voigt. Atheneum, 1986. ISBN 0-689-31202-4.
URL: www.scils.rutgers.edu/special/kay/voigt.html
Subjects: contemporary issues

Questions

1. In which book does a character's date drink too much before driving her home?

2. In which book does a character find she has nothing in common with her old friends after she's in an accident?

3. In which book does a girl who always says the wrong thing do everything right to help her friend recover from an accident?

4. In which book must a pretty, popular cheerleader adjust to being known as a cripple?

5. In which book does a girl finally learn to tell the truth instead of always being "nice"?

Jacob Have I Loved

Katherine Paterson. Harper, 1990. ISBN 0-06440368-8.
URL: www.ipl.org/youth/AskAuthor/paterson.html
Awards: Newbery
Study Guides: LL; Portals; Novel Units; LIFT; Sch.
Subjects: contemporary issues

Questions

1. In which book is a girl nicknamed "Wheeze"?

2. In which book does a pretty and talented character constantly push her sibling into the background?

3. In which book is Captain Hiram's house swept away in a hurricane?

4. In which book is Grandma always quoting the Bible?

5. In which book is one twin very envious of the younger one?

Jeremy Thatcher, Dragon Hatcher

Bruce Coville. Harcourt, 1992. ISBN 0-15-200748-2 (hc); ISBN 0-671-74782-7 (pb)
URL: www.brucecoville.com/

Study Guides: Novel Units
Subjects: fantasy

Questions

1. In which book does a character choose the Babylonian name Tiamet?

2. In which book does a pet animal eat chicken livers and drink gallons of milk?

3. In which book does a librarian make a gateway into another world using bits of eggshell, baby teeth, and the skin shed by an animal?

4. In which book does a character stumble into the magic shop of S. Elives?

5. In which book does a character get in trouble with his art teacher even though he loves to draw?

Jip: His Story

Katherine Paterson. Dutton, 1996. ISBN 0-525-67543-4.
URL: www.ipl.org/youth/AskAuthor/paterson.html
Subjects: historical fiction; prejudice

Questions

1. In which book does a character help his friend Sheldon build a cage for an idiot man?

2. In which book do a teacher and her Quaker fiancé help someone find his roots?

3. In which book does the main character learn his mother is a runaway slave and his father was her master?

4. In which book does a character refuse to escape to Canada without his lunatic friend?

5. In which book does a character find the stories of Uncle Tom's Cabin and Oliver Twist very meaningful?

Joey Pigza Swallowed the Key

Jack Gantos. Farrar, Straus and Giroux, 1998. ISBN 0-374-33664-4 (hc); ISBN 0-06-440833-7 (pb).
URL: www.publishersweekly.com/NBF/docs/porgantosbio.html
Subjects: contemporary issues; handicaps

Questions

1. In which book has a character passed from grade to grade because no teacher wants to have him for two years in a row?

2. In which book does a character grind up all the classroom pencils, then stick his finger in the sharpener?

3. In which book does a character think that shoofly pie is made of shoes and flies?

4. In which book does a character meet a teacher called Special Ed?

5. In which book does a character cut off the tip of a girl's nose when he trips while carrying the teacher's sharp scissors?

Johnny Tremain

Esther Forbes. Houghton Mifflin, 1943. ISBN 0-440-91100-1 (pb).
URL: www.mcdougallittell.com/lit/guest/forbes/index.htm
Awards: Newbery
Study Guides: LL; Portals; Lit. U.; Novel Units; Connect; Sch.
Subjects: historical fiction—American Revolution

Questions

1. In which book is a character's hand severely burned by a pot of molten silver?

2. In which book does a character belong to the "Sons of Liberty"?

3. In which book does a character carry secret messages to the Boston Patriots?

4. In which book is there a horse named Goblin?

5. In which book does a Rebel Yankee boy carry messages for the British?

Journey to an 800 Number

E.L. Konigsburg. Atheneum, 1982. ISBN 0-689-82679-6 (pb).
URL: www.edupaperback.org/authorbios/Konigsburg_EL.html
Awards: Newbery
Subjects: families

Questions

1. In which book does a boy's father own a camel named Ahmed?

2. In which book does a character spend a month with a camel keeper?

3. In which book does a character take a camel and go to shopping malls, conventions, state fairs, dude ranches, and night clubs?

4. In which book is a baby named "Rainbow" according to an old Indian custom?

5. In which book does someone meet a girl and her mother several times, under several names, and under several circumstances, while traveling to conventions with his father?

Journey to Topaz

Yoshiko Uchida. Creative Arts, 1995. ISBN 0-91687085-5 (pb).
URL: www.jps.net/gailhd/Hall_3.html
Subjects: historical fiction—World War II; Japanese-American; prejudice

Questions

1. In which book are all persons of Japanese descent ordered to leave their homes?

2. In which book is a family housed in a horse stall, which the soldiers insist is an apartment?

3. In which book is a camp for hundreds of people located on the Utah desert?

4. In which book does a character decide to join a special unit in the U.S. Army even though he has been treated as an alien?

5. In which book does a family have to go to a relocation camp?

Joyride

Gretchen Olson. Boyds Mill Press, 1998. ISBN 1-56397-687-0.
Subjects: contemporary issues; prejudice

Questions

1. In which book does a character have to work on a strawberry harvest as payback for driving around a bean field?

2. In which book does a character discover that individuals often differ from their stereotypes?

3. In which book do Mexican workers build a tennis court for someone so that he can practice?

4. In which book do the main characters discover who's been causing an outbreak of vandalism?

5. In which book do playing soccer and working hard help someone win a tennis trophy?

The Juggler

John Morressy. Holt, 1996. ISBN 0-8050-4217-2 (hc); ISBN 06-447174-8 (pb).
URL: www.sfsite.com/isfdb-bin/exact_author.cgi?John_Morressy
Notes: Mature theme
Subjects: historical fiction—Middle Ages

Questions

1. In which book does a peasant boy return home to find his village in ruins and everyone dead?

2. In which book does a performer lose a hand as punishment for displeasing an eccentric nobleman?

3. In which book is a character pursued from place to place by a black-clad stranger?

4. In which book does a traveling entertainer become the greatest performer in the world?

5. In which book does the devil try many deceitful ways to gain possession of a man's soul?

Julie of the Wolves

Jean Craighead George. Harper, 1972. ISBN 0-064-40058-1.
URL: www.jeancraigheadgeorge.com
Awards: Newbery
Study Guides: LL; Portals; Lit. U.; Novel Units; LIFT; Sch.;
Subjects: animals; journeys; Alaska

Questions

1. In which book does a character persuade some wolves to take her in as part of their family?

2. In which book does a thirteen-year-old girl cross the Alaskan tundra on foot?

3. In which book does a character behave submissively so that an animal family will adopt her?

4. In which book does a character use her Eskimo skills to help her survive alone?

5. In which book is a beloved animal killed by airborne hunters?

Julie's Wolf Pack

Jean Craighead George. HarperCollins, 1997. ISBN 0-06-440-721-7.
URL: www.jeancraigheadgeorge.com
Awards: Newbery
Subjects: animals; Alaska

Questions

1. In which book does a former clan leader joined a new group after his own entire clan has died of starvation?

2. In which book does a young leader face enemies both within and outside his clan?

3. In which book are territorial boundaries marked by scent?

4. In which book does the sun stay out all night?

5. In which book is a wild animal held captive and later returned to its wild home?

Just as Long as We're Together

Judy Blume. Bantam Doubleday Dell, 1991. ISBN 0-440-21094-1 (pb).
URL: www.judyblume.com/
Subjects: contemporary issues; families

Questions

1. In which book does a character find out that her new friend's mother is really a famous TV star?

2. In which book does Alison, a new Vietnamese girl, become the most popular fifth grader?

3. In which book does a character find out that it's okay to be a gullible optimist?

4. In which book does Stephanie find out that it's hard to be best friends with people who keep secrets?

5. In which book is a character surprised to find out that her parents have separated without telling her?

The Kidnappers

Willo Davis Roberts. Atheneum, 1997. ISBN 0-689-81394-5 (hc); ISBN 0-689-816393-7 (pb).
URL: www.cbcbooks.org/navigation/autindex.htm
Subjects: contemporary issues; mystery

Questions

1. In which book are students transported to and from school by limousines with chauffeurs?

2. In which book does a character hide from the school bully in the lobby of an apartment building?

3. In which book is a character's report of a serious crime not believed because of his reputation for telling exaggerated stories and tall tales?

4. In which book does a character help a police artist create a computer sketch of a dark-haired stranger wearing a gold earring?

5. In which book do two boys use lamps and a mirror to flash SOS signals from an apartment window?

The Killer's Cousin

Nancy Werlin. Delacorte, 1998. ISBN 0-385-32560-6 (hc); ISBN 440-22751-8 (pb).
URL: www.ala.org/booklist/v95/youth/se1/57werlin.html
Subjects: contemporary issues; mystery

Questions

1. In which book does a character tell the story of his second senior year in high school?

2. In which book does a character live in a third-floor apartment above his aunt and uncle?

3. In which book does someone erase a hard drive and glue CDs into their cases?

4. In which book does a character often hear humming and a voice asking him to "Help Lily"?

5. In which book does a character rescue someone from an attic fire that she herself has set?

King of the Wind

Marguerite Henry. Macmillan, 1990. ISBN 0-02-743629-2 (hc).
URL: www.modelhorses.com/mcf/mhenry.html
Awards: Newbery
Study Guides: Novel Units; LEAP
Subjects: animals

Questions

1. Which book is about an animal named Sham?

2. In which book is an animal named for the sun?

3. In which book are six stallions and six slave boys sent as a gift to the French Court?

4. In which book is a small colt fed camel's milk?

5. In which book do a stallion's offspring race to win the queen's plate?

The King's Shadow

Elizabeth Alder. Farrar, Straus and Giroux, 1995. ISBN 0-374-34182-6 (hc); ISBN 0-440-22011-4 (pb).
URL: www.powells.com/biblio/36400-36600/0440220114.html
Subjects: historical fiction—Middle Ages

Questions

1. In which book does a character who hopes to become a minstrel lose his tongue in a village brawl?

2. In which book does a character sell his nephew into slavery?

3. In which book are a raven and a three-tailed comet believed to be omens of misfortune?

4. In which book does a rescuer force the victim of a shipwreck to swear away his inheritance?

5. In which book is a squire forced to kill his lord's beloved brother?

Lassie Come-Home

Eric Knight. Holt, 1971, rev. ed. 1995. ISBN 0-8050-0721-0 (hc); ISBN 0-440-40760-5 (pb).
URL: www.members.aol.com/Chelcolly/Lassie.html
Subjects: animals, classic

Questions

1. In which book does a character allow a homesick dog to escape?

2. In which book does an elderly couple care for an animal, then allow it to continue its journey?

3. In which book does an animal journey from Scotland to England?

4. In which book does a father lose his job in a mine?

5. In which book does a pure-bred dog fight a weasel in order to eat his freshly killed rabbit?

The Last Safe Place on Earth

Richard Peck. Bantam Doubleday Dell, 1995. ISBN 0-4402-2007-6.
URL: http://ccpl.carr.lib.md.us/mae/peck-web.htm
Subjects: contemporary issues

Questions

1. In which book is a character in the same class in their new high school as his adopted sister?

2. In which book is a character attracted to his kid sister's new babysitter.

3. In which book does a child spoil her father's Halloween decorations because she's been told her Halloween celebrations are evil?

4. In which book does a family provide help for some of their son's friends?

5. In which book does a family discover that a so-called perfect community can still have problems?

The Legend of Jimmy Spoon

Kristiana Gregory. Harcourt, 1990. ISBN 0-15-243-22.
URL: www.kstrom.net/isk/books/middle/mi225.html
Subjects: historical fiction—WWII

Questions

1. In which book does a character resent having to work in his father's store just because he is the only son?

2. In which book does a Mormon boy decide to go off with the Indians in order to get a horse?

3. In which book is a white boy adopted by the Indian chief's old mother?

4. In which book does a character steal a feather from an eagle without doing the bird any harm?

5. In which book does a white boy scare off a grizzly bear, saving the life of a Shoshone?

The Library Card

Jerry Spinelli. Scholastic, 1997. ISBN 0-590-46731-X.
URL: www.carr.lib.md.us/authco/spinelli-j.htm
Subjects: fantasy; school stories

Questions

1. In which book does a character change his life when he discovers the book "I Wonder"?

2. In which book does a character discover she knows more about her favorite TV personalities than she does about herself?

3. In which book does a character hijack a bookmobile?

4. In which book does a character live in a 1976 Cadillac Eldorado with his uncle?

5. In which book does a blue card serve as the magical link between separate stories?

Lily's Crossing

Patricia Reilly Giff. Delacorte, 1997. ISBN 0-385-32142-2 (hc).
URL: www.oksba.com/1999-2000/childrens/lily's_crossing/lily.htm
Awards: Newbery
Subjects: historical fiction

Questions

1. In which book does a father send a secret message by writing a series of book titles?

2. In which book is a birthday present a key to an empty house?

3. In which book does a friendship start with the rescue of a cat from drowning?

4. In which book do paper stars remind someone of her dead mother?

5. In which book is a character worried about his sister Ruth, whom he last saw in France?

Lincoln, a Photobiography

Russell Freedman. Clarion, 1987. ISBN 0-395-51848-2 (hc); ISBN 0-89919-380-3 (pb).
URL: www.sdcoe.k12.ca.us/score/linc/linctg.html
Awards: Newbery
Study Guides: Novel Units
Subjects: biography

Questions

1. In which book can you see a photograph of a president's own copy book?

2. In which book does a man save a newspaper clipping referring to him as a man of "grand simplicity of purpose"?

3. In which book is finding capable wartime generals a problem for a president?

4. In which book is a man called "pigeon-hearted," because he prefers pardoning prisoners to executing them?

5. In which book is a president elected by the votes of the Northern states alone?

The Lion, the Witch, and the Wardrobe

C.S. Lewis. Macmillan 1950. HarperCollins, 1994. ISBN 0-06-023482-2 (hc); ISBN 0-06-447104-7 (pb).
URL: www.cslewis.drzeus.net/
Study Guides: Portals; Lit. U.; Novel Units; LEAP; Sch.
Subjects: fantasy, classic

Questions

1. In which book does a character rule a country where it is "always winter and never Christmas"?

2. In which book are some characters called "sons of Adam" or "daughters of Eve"?

3. In which book are stone statues restored to life by an act of sacrifice?

4. In which book does someone betray his brother and sisters after he eats Turkish Delight given him by the white witch?

5. In which book is evil conquered by "deep magic from before the dawn of time"?

Little Men

Louisa May Alcott. Dover, 1997. ISBN 0-48629-8051.
URL: www.alcottweb.com/
Subjects: classic; historical fiction; school stories

Questions

1. In which book do Professor Bhaer and his wife run a school for boys?

2. In which book does a family care for a homeless street musician and his friend?

3. In which book is a character told to leave school because he's taught others to drink, swear, smoke, and play poker?

4. In which book do some children get lost while picking huckleberries?

5. In which book does a character take the blame for stealing some money, even though he knows who is the culprit?

The Little Prince

Antoine De Saint-Exupery. Harcourt, 1971. ISBN 0-15-625-28207.
URL: www.inteligente.com/b612/yes.htm
Study Guides: LL
Subjects: classic; fantasy

Questions

1. In which book does a character draw a picture of a boa constructor digesting an elephant?

2. In which book does a character love his flower?

3. In which book does the main character meet a lot of strange grownups, such as the businessman who counts all the stars he thinks he owns?

4. In which book does a pilot meet a prince from asteroid B-612?

5. In which book is an asteroid in danger from baobob trees?

Little Women

Louisa May Alcott. Penguin, 1994. ISBN 0-14-036668-7.
URL: www.alcottweb.com/
Subjects: classic; historical fiction

Questions

1. In which book does a character climb trees and ride horses, instead of acting like a lady?

2. In which book does someone fall in love with Laurie?

3. In which book does one sister write a poem about another sister being missed after she dies?

4. In which book does a character sell her hair for $25.00 to help her ill father?

5. Which book is about the activities of a family while their father fighting in the Civil War?

A Long Way from Chicago

Richard Peck. Dial, 1998. ISBN 0-8037-2290-7.
URL: www.penguinputnam.com/catalog/yreader/authors/2237_biography.html
Awards: Newbery
Subjects: families

Questions

1. In which book do the Cowgills boys destroy mailboxes and outhouses?

2. In which book does Grandma use very smelly cheese as bait for the catfish?

3. In which book does a character help some lovers elope by pretending to be the

Phantom Brakeman?

4. In which book do the stories about Shotgun Cheatham grow bigger after a reporter comes to town?

5. In which book does a character embarrass her brother by tap dancing in the streets?

Lyddie

Katherine Paterson. Dutton, 1991. ISBN 0-525-67338-5.
URL: www.ipl.org/youth/AskAuthor/paterson.html
Study Guides: LL; Novel Units
Subjects: historical fiction

Questions

1. In which book does a character find a runaway slave hiding in their old cabin?

2. In which book does a character find that working in a mill pays far better than working for an innkeeper?

3. In which book does a character have to lease out the farm, move in with her sister, and find jobs for her children when the father disappears?

4. In which book does a character work so hard she becomes very miserly?

5. In which book does a character learn to read by pasting up pages on her loom?

M. C. Higgins, the Great

Virginia Hamilton. Maxwell Macmillan, 1988. ISBN 0-68971-694-X.
URL: www.virginiahamilton.com/
Awards: Newbery
Study Guides: LL
Subjects: families

Questions

1. In which book does someone dream that his mother will become a country music star?

2. In which book does the main character spend hours sitting on top of a 40-foot pole outside his house?

3. In which book is a coal slag heap moving down the mountain?

4. In which book does a character trap and hunt rabbits to help feed his family when his father isn't working?

5. Which book is about Mayo Cornelius?

Make Lemonade

Virginia Euwer Wolff. Scholastic, 1993. ISBN 0-590-48141-X.
URL: http://literacy.kent.edu/Oasis/Pubs/0300-17.html
Subjects: contemporary issues

Questions

1. In which book does someone decide to baby-sit for a single mom?

2. In which book does a mother insist her daughter must go to college?

3. In which book does a fourteen year old girl help a seventeen year old get her life together?

4. In which book does a character use her knowledge of CPR to save a baby?

5. In which book does a letter to a billionaire in a newspaper bring $5.00 and a promise of more if the character shows some tenacity?

Maniac Magee

Jerry Spinelli. Harper Trophy, 1992. ISBN 0-06-440-4242.
URL: www.carr.lib.md.us/authco/spinelli-j.htm
Awards: Newbery
Study Guides: LL; Portals; Lit. U.; Novel Units; LEAP; RBB; Sch.
Subjects: contemporary issues; humor

Questions

1. Who won a year's worth of pizzas by untying the famous cobble's knot?

2. In which book does a homeless boy sleep in the zoo with the deer and the buffalo?

3. In which book did a character decide to change a bully's name from Mars Bar to Snickers?

4. In which book did a character find homes and acceptance with the black kids from the East End and also the white kids from the West End?

5. In which book did someone tell about the time he struck out Willie Mays?

Mariel of Redwall

Brian Jacques. Philomel, 1992. ISBN 0-399-22144-1 (hc); ISBN 0-380-71922-3 (pb).
URL: www.redwall.org/dave/jacques.html
Subjects: animals; fantasy; strong female

Questions

1. In which book does a castaway call herself "Storm" because she was washed up from the sea?

2. In which book does a feast include raspberry cream pudding, mushroom cress soup, and hazelnut crumble?

3. In which book has a great bell inscribed with runes been stolen by pirates?

4. In which book does a ship's crew drag their vessel up-river to hide it in the forest?

5. In which book does a party of travelers find their way by following the directions in an ancient rhyme?

Megan's Island

Willo Davis Roberts. Aladdin, 1990. ISBN 0-689-13878
URL: http://mirror.lps.org/instruction/gifted/Curr/samp55.html#megan
Subjects: adventure; mystery

Questions

1. In which book is a character upset because she's not allowed to tell anyone where they've moved?

2. In which book is a character scared when she finds out that a strange man is pretending to be the uncle of two red-headed kids?

3. In which book does a character find a birth certificate for someone named Margaret Anne and realize that it must be her own?

4. In which book do some children hide in their island tree house when they find a stranger looking for them?

5. In which book does a character begin to wonder why her mother changes jobs and towns so often?

The Midwife's Apprentice

Karen Cushman. HarperCollins, 1995. ISBN 0-06-440630-X.
URL: www.ipl.org/youth/AskAuthor/cushmanbio.html
Awards: Newbery
Study Guides: LL; Portals; Novel Units; LIFT
Subjects: historical fiction—Middle Ages

Questions

1. In which book does a merchant give Beetle an ivory comb, a wink, and a compliment—which leads her to choose another name for herself?

2. In which book do fake devil tracks lead the villagers to find out embarrassing truths about every one who's picked on a vagabond girl?

3. In which book does a character sleep in a rotting garbage heap because it's warm?

4. In which book does a scholar teach someone to read by pretending to teach her cat?

5. In which book does someone learn she should "try and risk and fail and try again" without giving up?

Missing May

Cynthia Rylant. Dell, 1993. ISBN 0-440-40865-2.
URL: http://falcon.jmu.edu/~ramseyil/rylant.htm
Awards: Newbery
Study Guides: LL;Portals; Novel Units; LIFT
Subjects: contemporary issues

Questions

1. In which book does a character go to live with some old people in a rusty antiquated trailer?

2. In which book does a character feel right at home when she sees her new house has lots of whirligigs and chocolate milk?

3. In which book is there someone who collects pictures from cereal boxes, tin cans, old circulars, and anything else he can find?

4. In which book does a character find peace in the swoop of an owl's wings?

5. In which book do some characters set out to visit a Small Medium At Large, who is also known as the Bat Lady?

The Moorchild

Eloise McGraw. Simon & Schuster, 1996. ISBN 0-689-80654-X.
URL: http://henson2.ssu.edu/~elbond/moor.htm
Awards: Newbery
Subjects: fantasy

Questions

1. In which book is a character banned from the fairy folk because she cannot hide herself?

2. In which book does a character discover she already knows how to play the bagpipes?

3. In which book is someone befriended by Tam, the tinker's helper?

4. In which book does a grandmother use a monk's old books to teach a child how to read?

5. In which book does a character put an ointment in somebody's eye so it will see fairy land as it is without imaginary glamour?

Mrs. Frisby and the Rats of NIMH

Robert O' Brien. Simon & Schuster, 1999. ISBN 0-689-829663.
URL: www.radiks.net/~camoon/rcob/rcobfaq.htm
Awards: Newbery
Study Guides: LL; Lit. U.; Novel Units; LIFT; RBB
Subjects: animals

Questions

1. In which book does a crow fly off with two mice clinging to his beak?

2. In which book do some animals use their ability to read in order to escape their cages?

3. In which book does a character help create a city complete with electricity?

4. Which is the title of the book about the National Institute of Mental Health?

5. In which book does a widowed mouse seek help from some wise rats?

My Louisiana Sky

Kimberly Willis Holt. Holt, 1998. ISBN 0-8050-5251-8 (hc); ISBN 0-440-41570-5 (pb).
URL: www.kimberlyholt.com/
Subjects: contemporary issues; twentieth century

Questions

1. In which book is a character taunted because her mother is mentally disabled?

2. In which book does a character receive her first kiss when she is not invited to a swimming party?

3. In which book does a character cut her long hair so she can look like Audrey Hepburn?

4. In which book does a grandmother have a heart attack as she is picking green beans?

5. In which book does a slow-thinking man save some rare plants by predicting a hurricane?

Night Journey

Kathryn Lasky. Puffin, 1986. ISBN 0-14-032048-2.
URL: www.xensei.com/users/newfilm/homelsk.htm
Subjects: contemporary issues; historical fiction

Questions

1. In which book does a family pretend to be actors in a play in order to move from town to town?

2. In which book does a character live with her mother, grandmother, and great-grandmother?

3. In which book do we learn about the history of dehumanizing people by talking about their differences in order to make killing them easier?

4. In which book is gold smuggled out of the country in cookies?

5. In which book do we read two stories at once, one happening today and one happening 80 years ago?

Nightjohn

Gary Paulsen. Delacorte, 1993. ISBN 0-385-30838-8.
URL: www.trelease-on-reading.com/paulsen.html
Subjects: historical fiction

Questions

1. In which book does a character try to learn things by listening under the windows of the big house?

2. In which book does the master hitch up a slave woman as if she were a horse?

3. In which book does a slave return to the south to help teach others to read?

4. In which book does a character trade tobacco in return for learning the alphabet?

5. In which book does the master delight in whipping his slaves in the springhouse?

Nothing but the Truth

Avi. Orchard, 1991. ISBN 0-531-05595-6.
URL: www.avi-writer.com/QandA.html
Awards: Newbery
Study Guides: LL; Novel Units
Subjects: school stories

Questions

1. In which book do we see the "truth" from many points of view?

2. In which book does a boy's attitude indicate that rules are for other people?

3. In which book does the father's habit of acting without all the necessary information cause trouble for his son and the whole school?

4. In which book do we discover that outrageous ideas sell newspapers but that rational explanations are not newsworthy?

5. In which book does a character's self-confidence stem from his ability in track and his role as class clown?

Old Yeller

Fred Gipson. Harper Trophy, 1990. ISBN 0-06-440-3823.
URL: http://rampages.onramp.net/~classics/8_oyell.htm
Awards: Newbery
Subjects: animals, classics

Questions

1. In which book does an animal get hurt by a wild pig?

2. In which book does someone find that his hound dog is also a good hog dog?

3. In which book does a character have to shoot his pet after it's been attacked by a killer wolf?

4. Which book is about a family living on Birdsong Creek?

5. In which book does a character adopt a thieving hound?

On My Honor

Marion Bauer. Dell, 1987. ISBN 0-440-46633-4.
URL: www.randomhouse.com/teachers/guides/onmy.html
Awards: Newbery
Study Guides: SG; LL
Subjects: contemporary issues; grief and death

Questions

1. In which book does a character keep quiet about the drowning of his best friend?

2. In which book does a boy's best friend die after the boy breaks a promise to his father?

3. In which book does one character bet another about swimming out to a sandbar?

4. In which book does a character find himself usually doing what his friend wants to do, rather than the things he wants to do himself?

5. In which book does the title refer to the promises made to a father?

Out of the Dust

Karen Hesse. Scholastic, 1997. ISBN 0-590-36080-9.
URL: www.riverdale.k12.or.us/~cmaxwell/hesse.htm

Awards: Newbery
Subjects: historical fiction—Great Depression

Questions

1. In which book does a character love playing the piano in a band with Arley Wanderle and Mad Dog?

2. Which book is a story about the Depression years told in short, free verse poems?

3. In which book does a father cause a horrible accident when he leaves a pail of kerosene by the wood stove?

4. In which book does a character relearn how to play the piano again after her hands are terribly burned?

5. In which book does a teacher let a migrant family live in her classroom until their new baby is born?

Over Sea, Under Stone

Susan Cooper. Collier, 1989. ISBN 0-02042-7859.
URL: www.puffin.co.uk/living/aut_10.html
Subjects: fantasy

Questions

1. In which book does an uncle represent Merlin?

2. In which book does the mysterious Mr. Withers prove to be one of the forces of evil?

3. In which book does an uncle enlist the children in representing the forces of good?

4. In which book do the characters find the Holy Grail?

5. In which book do some youngsters find an old map in an attic?

Petey

Ben Mikaelson. Hyperion, 1998. ISBN 0-7868-2376-3.
URL: www.benmikaelsen.com/books_petey.htm
Subjects: friendship; handicaps

Questions

1. In which book does a boy grow to manhood and live his entire life in institutions?

2. In which book is a character assumed to be an idiot because he lacks mobility and speech?

3. In which book does Trevor find friendship in the most unlikely place of all?

4. In which book does a handicapped man take over the parenting role from too-busy parents?

5. In which book do two handicapped children have fun playing cowboys with each other?

The Phantom Tollbooth

Norton Juster. Bullseye Books, 1961. ISBN 0-3948-2037-1.
URL: www3.sympatico.ca/alanbrown/kids.htm
Study Guides: LL; Portals; Lit. U.; LEAP; Novel Units
Subjects: classic; fantasy

Questions

1. In which book does a boy travel through "The Valley of Sound," "Dictionopolis," and "Digitopolis"?

2. In which book do we find an animal with the body of an alarm clock?

3. In which book does a boy get hungrier as he eats more Subtraction Stew?

4. In which book is there a Dodecahedron, a character with twelve faces?

5. In which book is there a "Castle in the Air"?

The Pinballs

Betsy Byars. Harper & Row, 1977. ISBN 0-06-440198-7.
URL: www.betsybyars.com/
Study Guides: LL; Portals; Novel Units; LIFT; RBB
Subjects: contemporary issues; families

Questions

1. Which book is about a character who's been beaten by her stepfather?

2. In which book does a character say his legs were broken in a football game rather than admit the injury was caused by his father?

3. In which book was one of the main characters left in front of a farmhouse and raised by two elderly twins?

4. In which book is a puppy smuggled into a hospital as a birthday present?

5. In which book does someone make a list of "Bad Things That Have Happened To Me" and "Gifts I Got That I Didn't Want"?

The Place of Lions

Eric Campbell. Harcourt, 1991. ISBN 0-15-200371-1.
URL: www.powells.com/biblio/12400-12600/0152003711.html
Subjects: contemporary issues; other lands

Questions

1. In which book do we have a plane crash over the Serengeti Plain?

2. In which book do we meet an aging animal who is being challenged for his leadership role by a younger male?

3. In which book is a character used as a possible meal by a mother teaching her young to stalk their prey?

4. In which book do we feel hatred at the slaughter of animals so that man might use their tusks and horns?

5. In which book does the fate of two wounded men depend on a teenage boy?

Poppy

Avi. Orchard, 1995. ISBN 0-3807-2769-2
URL: www.avi-writer.com/QandA.html
Subjects: animals; fantasy

Questions

1. In which book does disaster strike when two sweethearts walk out in the moonlight without permission?

2. In which book does a large animal family need a new home when it outgrows its food supply?

3. In which book is an old Log Cabin Syrup can used as a special secret place?

4. In which book does a character learn that her family is misinformed about their supposed worst enemy?

5. In which book does a heroine fight for her life with a porcupine quill?

Preacher's Boy

Katherine Paterson. Clarion, 1999. ISBN 0-395-86897-5 (hc).
URL: www.ipl.org/youth/AskAuthor/paterson.html
Subjects: families; historical fiction

Questions

1. In which book do two boys steal someone's bloomers and run them up the flagpole?

2. In which book does a character nearly drown someone who sinks his clothes in a swimming hole?

3. In which book do some characters use raspberry juice to write a kidnap note?

4. In which book does a character's dream of riding in a motorcar unexpectedly come true?

5. In which book do a boy and his father ring in the new year and the twentieth century?

Quest for a Maid

Frances Mary Hendry. Farrar, Straus and Giroux, 1992.
     ISBN 0-374-46155-4.
URL: www.home.earthlink.net/~zzz12/index.htm
Subjects: historical fiction

Questions

1. In which book is a nine-year-old betrothed to a six-year-old because she is the only one who can understand his speech?

2. In which book does a character try to save her sister Inge from being tried for witchcraft?

3. In which book does a character save the life of the Norwegian princess who is to become Queen of the Scots?

4. In which book does a character with speech problems, due to a harelip, learn to read and write in several languages?

5. In which book does someone run away from having his foot cut off as a punishment? He's saved because the lord doesn't know his name.

The Rain Catchers

Jean Thesman. William Morrow/Avon, 1992. ISBN 0-380-71711-5.
Subjects: contemporary issues

Questions

1. In which book is the rainwater from the honeysuckle vine collected in jars?

2. In which book do the tea time stories of family and friends show that sometimes everyone makes mistakes and becomes frightened and embarrassed?

3. In which book does Grandmother take the hands off all her clocks so that she only hears the hours?

4. In which book do the ashes of a character and her dog, Gip, get a sea burial?

5. In which book does Grandmother's house have plenty of room for family and friends to live there?

The Ramsay Scallop

Frances Temple. Orchard, 1994. ISBN 0-531-08686-0.
URL: www.intercraze.com/eind/0064406016
Subjects: historical fiction; journeys

Questions

1. In which book do people fear that the turn of the new century will bring the end of the world?

2. In which book does a character welcome the chance to travel with a man she doesn't like, just because she wants to leave home?

3. In which book do six girls climb 130 stone steps on their knees?

4. In which book does a young knight come back from the Crusades feeling disappointed with himself and his calling as a fighter?

5. In which book does someone trade his beloved stallion for water for his people, while another character sells her favorite horse so that a needy family can buy a house?

Rascal: A Memoir of a Better Era

Sterling North. Houghton Mifflin, 1995. ISBN 0-395-73253-0
URL: www.sterlingnorth.com/history/
Awards: Newbery
Study Guides: Novel Units
Subjects: animals

Questions

1. In which book does a pet raccoon ride in a bicycle basket?

2. In which book does a pet raccoon have to be locked up after raiding the neighborhood for sweet corn?

3. In which book does a St. Bernard dig a baby animal out of a tree stump?

4. In which book does a character build a canoe in the living room?

5. In which book does a character have pet skunks, woodchucks, cats, a raccoon, and a crow?

Reaching Dustin

Vicki Grove. Putnam, 1998. ISBN 0-399-23008-4.
URL: www.penguinputnam.com/cgi-bin/to_catalog.cgi?section=catalog&page=yadult/authors/676_biography.html
Subjects: school stories

Questions

1. In which book a character advised to walk a mile in someone's shoes before judging him?

2. In which book does a character try to mend an old wound by writing and publishing a story?

3. In which book is the Confederate flag tattooed on the male members of the family?

4. In which book does a Civil War period tunnel become a sanctuary for a troubled character?

5. In which book can a character make beautiful music, but in order to shut out the world, he doesn't speak?

Red Scarf Girl: A Memoir of the Cultural Revolution

Ji-Li Jiang. HarperCollins, 1997. ISBN 0-06-027585-5 (hc); ISBN 0-06-446208-0 (pb).
URL: www.harperchildrens.com/schoolhouse/TeachersGuides/redscarf.htm
Subjects: contemporary issues; other lands; strong female

Questions

1. In which book is a character denied a chance to audition for a special dance team because, her grandfather was a landlord?

2. In which book are students encouraged to defy their teachers and make accusations against them?

3. In which book are family photographs burned because they show people wearing old-fashioned clothing?

4. In which book is a city girl required to re-mold herself by going to work in the rice paddies?

5. In which book does a cat reveal an incriminating letter by scratching in her litter box?

Redwall

Brian Jacques. Putnam, 1987. ISBN 0-399-21424-0.
URL: www.redwall.org/dave/jacques.html
Subjects: fantasy

Questions

1. In which book does a character discover his name is an anagram for "I am that is"?

2. In which book does an animal character plot to take over the abbey in a wood?

3. In which book does a character convert the enemy sparrows into becoming part of his invading army?

4. In which book does a snake guard the sword that once belonged to a famous warrior?

5. In which book does the reader meet good and evil characters such as Silent Sam, Basil Stag Hare, Warbeak, Chicken Hound, and Dark Claw?

Rifles for Watie

Harold Keith. Crowell, 1991. ISBN 0-690-04907-2.
URL: http://title3.sde.state.ok.us/literatureanda/harold.htm
Awards: Newbery
Study Guides: LL; Lit. U.; Novel Units
Subjects: historical fiction—Civil War

Questions

1. In which book does a character join the Union Army after his family is attacked by Missouri bushwhackers?

2. In which book does an army captain harass a volunteer soldier because of his name?

3. In which book does a Cherokee colonel lead a Rebel Cavalry unit?

4. In which book does a soldier confiscate a woman's only milk cow and then return it to her after dark?

5. In which book does a Union scout find himself a member of the Rebel Army?

Roll of Thunder, Hear My Cry

Mildred Taylor. Dial, 1976. ISBN 0-8037-7473-7.
URL: http://falcon.jmu.edu/~ramseyil/taylor.htm
Awards: Newbery
Study Guides: LL; Portals; Lit. U.; Novel Units; RBB; Sch.
Subjects: families; prejudice

Questions

1. In which book is a family resented only because they are black?

2. In which book do the black children have to dodge a school bus full of white children every day?

3. In which book do the black children have to use the worn-out textbooks discarded from the white schools?

4. In which book does a teacher lose her job when the black families boycott a white-owned store?

5. In which book do the black children have to walk to school because they are not allowed to ride the school bus?

The Root Cellar

Janet Lunn. Scribner's, 1983. ISBN 0-684-17855-9 (hc); ISBN 0-14-038036-1 (pb).
URL: www.sunsite.utk.edu/civil-war/warweb.html
Awards: Newbery
Subjects: fantasy; historical fiction—Civil War

Questions

1. In which book is a character sent to live with her aunt and four cousins after her grandmother dies in Paris?

2. In which book does a character go back in time and exchange friendship tokens with a girl of a hundred years ago?

3. In which book does a Canadian run away with his American cousin to fight in the Civil War?

4. In which book do two characters walk most of the way from Albany to New York City after they lose their train tickets and their money?

5. In which book does a character cook an old-fashioned Christmas dinner for her family with help from a friend out of the past?

The Ruby in the Smoke

Philip Pullman. Knopf, 1985. ISBN 0-394-89589-4.
URL: www.puffin.co.uk/living/aut_41.html
       www.achuka.co.uk/ppsg.htm
Subjects: historical fiction; mystery

Questions

1. In which book does a character find she has a different father than the one she thought?

2. In which book does a character find a clue in a nightmare that she's had since childhood?

3. In which book do a young photographer and his actress sister come to someone's rescue?

4. In which book does the gift of a maharajah's jewel bring violence and death to the receivers?

5. In which book is there a curse of the "Seven Blessings"?

Run Away Home

Patricia McKissack. Scholastic, 1997. ISBN 0-590-46752-2.
URL: http://teacher.scholastic.com/authorsandbooks/authors/mckiss/bio.htm

Questions

1. In which book do Apaches work alongside and share recipes with former slaves?

2. In which book is Booker T. Washington's Tuskegee School introduced?

3. In which book do we learn about the Knights of the Southern Order of Manhood?

4. In which book do we learn that President Andrew Jackson freed all the black men who fought with him in the war?

5. In which book does the talk of clean and unclean food lead you to think it might be better to eat rats than pigs?

The Runaways

Zilpha Keatley Snyder. Delacorte, 1999. ISBN 0-385-32599-1 (hc).
URL: www.microweb.com/lsnyder/
Subjects: contemporary issues; historical fiction

Questions

1. In which book are a character and her mother trapped in the desert town of Rattler Springs?

2. In which book does an inherited cattle ranch appear to be worthless desert?

3. In which book is a character impatient with her mother for reading romance novels and watching soap operas?

4. In which book does a character read stories to the non-reading child next door?

5. In which book does a bus driver refuse to let three children on-board because no adult is with them?

Running Out of Time

Margaret Peterson Haddix. Simon & Schuster, 1995. ISBN 0-6898-3860-3.
URL: www.cla-net.org/groups/cyrm/sum/mj98haddix.html
Subjects: mystery

Questions

1. In which book does a character discover that she doesn't live in 1840, but in 1996?

2. In which book must a character escape from her village and travel alone in an unfamiliar world?

3. In which book does a character telephone a man for help, only to have him kidnap her?

4. In which book is a diphtheria epidemic caused by unethical scientists?

5. In which book does a character find that the mirrors in every house and building in town are actually windows into village life?

Sandry's Book

Tamora Pierce. Scholastic, 1997. ISBN 0-590-55356-9.
URL: www.sff.net/people/Tamora.Pierce/
Subjects: fantasy

Questions

1. In which book do four children, all strangers, find themselves together in a house called "Discipline"?

2. In which book does Roach discover he has the magic of growing plants?

3. In which book does a character save her friends from being buried by an earthquake, in spite of her fear of the dark?

4. In which book does a character find that her talent is in metal working, even though her family is opposed to her working in any craft?

5. In which book does a character find she can't control her magical gift?

Sasquatch

Roland Smith. Hyperion, 1998. ISBN 0-7868-0368-1.
URL: www.rolandsmith.com/
    An online study guide can be obtained at www.rolandsmith.com
Subjects: adventure

Questions

1. In which book does a character's father like to tinker with crazy ideas?

2. In which book do the lava tubes on Mt. St. Helens hide an underground lake?

3. In which book are the main characters students of cryptozoology?

4. In which book does the trunk that Buck calls "Pandora's Box" hide a trap door?

5. In which book does a large animal help a character save his injured father after a volcano erupts?

Save Queen of Sheba

Louise Moeri. Puffin, 1994. ISBN 0-1403-1486.
URL: www.nps.gov/whmi/educate.htm
Subjects: historical fiction—The West, survival

Questions

1. In which book does a character have to decide whether to stay in the shelter of a cave, or try to set out and find the trail of the other wagons?

2. In which book does a character rescue his lost sister from an Indian woman?

3. In which book is a character nearly scalped during a Sioux Indian raid?

4. In which book does a character find that he and his sister are the only survivors of an Indian attack on their wagon train?

5. In which book is a character tempted to stop looking for his lost little sister?

Scorpions

Walter Dean Myers. HarperCollins, 1988. ISBN 0-06-447066-0.
URL: www.scils.rutgers.edu/special/kay/myers.html
    http://teacher.scholastic.com/authorsandbooks/authors/myers/bio.htm
Awards: Newbery
Study Guides: LL; Novel Units; LIFT
Subjects: contemporary issues

Questions

1. In which book do we see into the life of a character who is trying to stay away from gangs and drugs?

2. In which book is a 12 year old asked to take his big brother's place as head of a gang?

3. In which book is a character kicked out of his house because he has hidden a gun there?

4. In which book do we feel how hard it is to earn enough money to get your brother out of jail?

5. In which book does a friend save a character's life by shooting his attackers?

Search for the Shadowman

Joan Lowrey Nixon. Bantam Doubleday Dell, 1997. ISBN 0-440-41128-9.
URL: www.members.aol.com/NikkiB5130/JNixon5130.htm
    http://teacher.scholastic.com/authorsandbooks/authors/nixon/bio.htm (Note: includes a project for students on writing mysteries.)
Subjects: mystery

Questions

1. In which book does a school assignment lead a character to understand a feud between his own great-aunt and his best friend's great-grandmother?

2. In which book does a character contact a college professor through the Internet for help with a school project?

3. In which book is a character faced with the dilemma that proving the honesty of a dead relative will bring disgrace on his best friend's family?

4. In which book is a family member identified by a horseshoe nail and a necklace made from a leather thong?

5. In which book do copies of love letters sent almost a hundred years ago help solve a mystery?

Searching for Candlestick Park

Peg Kehret. Dutton, 1997. ISBN 0-525-65256-6.
URL: www.pioneerdrama.com/playwrights/pk.html
Subjects: families; journeys; survival

Questions

1. In which book does a character run away when his mom says she's going to take his cat to the pound?

2. In which book does a character dream of joining his divorced father—another baseball fan?

3. In which book is someone so hungry that he eats all the leftover food from the trays at McDonald's?

4. In which book is Foxey the most important creature in a character's life?

5. In which book does a character learn that sometimes you have to trade in dreams for others that you can make happen by yourself?

The Secret of Sarah Revere

Ann Rinaldi. Harcourt, 1995. ISBN 0-15-200393-2.
URL: www.scils.rutgers.edu/special/kay/rinaldi.html
Subjects: historical fiction

Questions

1. In which book does a character find herself torn between her own opinion and her sister's opinion of her stepmother?

2. Which book is about the daughter of a famous American patriot?

3. In which book does a character's father keep the secret of who fired the first shot at Lexington?

4. In which book does a character learn that sometimes it's too late to make up with a friend?

5. In which book does a character give a book of poetry to a doctor when he leaves for a battle?

Secret of the Andes

Ann Nolan Clark. Puffin, 1976. ISBN 0-14-030926-8.
Awards: Newbery
Subjects: classic, other lands

Questions

1. In which book is there an old Inca llama herder?

2. In which book is there a character who wears golden plugs in his ears?

3. In which book does a character learn how to train his pet llama to carry burdens?

4. In which book does a character live in a hidden valley with only an old herder and some llamas?

5. Which book is supposed to be about a modern Inca?

The Secret of the Ruby Ring

Yvonne MacGrory. Milkweed, 1991. ISBN 0-915943-92-1 (pb).
URL: www.ivillage.com/books/articles/0,3359,50571~726,00.html
Subjects: fantasy/time travel

Questions

1. In which book does a character receive a magic present for her eleventh birthday?

2. In which book does a character learn that life in a big house is pleasant for the wealthy but harsh for the servants?

3. In which book is a character accused of stealing a piece of jewelry that is really her own?

4. In which book does a character see portraits of long-ago friends when she visits an old mansion near her home?

5. In which book does her memory of Irish history help a character escape the past and return to her own time?

Shabanu: Daughter of the Wind

Suzanne Fisher Staples. Knopf, 1989. ISBN 0-679-81030-7.
URL: www.indiana.edu/~eric_rec/ieo/bibs/staples.html
    www.ridgenet.org/event/staples.htm
Awards: Newbery
Study Guides: LL; LIFT
Subjects: families; other lands

Questions

1. Which book takes place in the Cholistan Desert of Pakistan?

2. In which book does a character bring forth a baby camel from its dying mother?

3. In which book does a character look forward to her arranged marriage?

4. In which book does a family move periodically as water wells dry up?

5. In which book is a man slain as he tries to protect his betrothed from an evil land-lord?

Shade's Children

Garth Nix. HarperCollins, 1997. ISBN 0-06-02782-4.
URL: www.eidolon.net/garth_nix/
Notes: Mature theme
Subjects: science fiction

Questions

1. In which book are children's brains removed at age 14 and used to manufacture robotic creatures?

2. In which book do young people escaping captivity find refuge in an old submarine?

3. In which book is a group of teenagers sent out to infiltrate a fortress and steal enemy secrets?

4. In which book do some characters rescue a friend from death in the Meat Factory?

5. In which book does the personality of a former scientist operate through a computer?

Shades of Gray

Carolyn Reeder. Simon & Schuster, 1989. ISBN 0-689-82696-6 (pb).
URL: www.childrensbookguild.org/reeder.html
Awards: Newbery
Study Guides: LL; Portals; LIFT; Novel Units
Subjects: historical fiction

Questions

1. In which book does an orphaned city boy go to live with his mother's back country family after the Civil War ends?

2. In which book are country people short of food because soldiers have looted their farms during the war years?

3. In which book does a character make peace with his worst enemy by offering to take a beating?

4. In which book is a ten-year-old girl unable to read because there has been no teacher for the school during war time?

5. In which book does a character learn that refusing to fight may take more courage than going to war?

Shadow Spinner

Susan Fletcher. Atheneum, 1998. ISBN 0-689-81852-1.
URL: www.wickespro.com/sale/0689818521
      www.cyberiran.com/history
Subjects: other lands

Questions

1. In which book does a mother deliberately maim her daughter in order to save her life?

2. In which book does a character's ability to tell stories put her in danger?

3. In which book do two girls escape from the palace inside the oil jars?

4. In which book does the Khatun fear and control all the women around her?

5. In which book is a blind storyteller really a sighted and important official?

The Shakespeare Stealer

Gary Blackwood. Dutton, 1998. ISBN 0-525-45863-8.
URL: www.redrival.com/mowrites4kids/blackwood/
Subjects: historical fiction

Questions

1. In which book is an apprentice taught a secret shorthand writing called "charactery"?

2. In which book is a character sold for 10 pounds by his master?

3. In which book does a character hide above a stage and cause the theater to be set afire?

4. In which book are women forbidden to act on the stage?

5. In which book does a dying man pull off his disguise to reveal a well-known person underneath?

Shiloh

Phyllis Naylor. Atheneum, 1991. ISBN 0-689-31614-3 (hc); ISBN 0-88122-911-3 (pb).
URL: www.ipl.org/youth/AskAuthor/Naylor.html
Awards: Newbery
Study Guides: LL; LEAP; Lit. U.; Novel Units; Portals; RBB; Sch.
Subjects: animals

Questions

1. In which book does a character promise to work for someone he dislikes, even after the person says he won't keep his side of the bargain?

2. In which book does a character find a dog who won't come when he's called, although he answers to a whistle?

3. In which book does a character spend hours collecting bottles and cans, so he won't have to return a dog to his abusive owner?

4. In which book does a character hide some of his own food each day so he can feed a hidden dog?

5. In which book does a German shepherd brutally attack a penned-up dog?

Shiloh Season

Phyllis Naylor. Atheneum, 1991. ISBN 0-689-31614-3.
URL: www.ipl.org/youth/AskAuthor/Naylor.html
Awards: Newbery
Study Guides: LEAP
Subjects: animals

Questions

1. In which book does a dog save the life of a man he dislikes?

2. In which book are the children told to stay away from a meadow where someone is poaching?

3. In which book does one character change another's behavior by writing letters to him?

4. In which book does a teacher have children think about the difference between truth and gossip?

5. In which book do two characters watch a neighbor shooting squirrels?

The Sign of the Beaver

Elizabeth Speare. Houghton Mifflin, 1983, 1995. ISBN 0-395-33890-5.
URL: www.indiana.edu/~eric_rec/ieo/bibs/speare.html
Awards: Newbery
Study Guides: LL; Portals; Lit. U.; Novel Units; LIFT; RBB
Subjects: historical fiction

Questions

1. In which book does a stranger steal someone's only means of getting food?

2. In which book is a character left alone in the new cabin while his father goes back to get his mother and the new baby?

3. In which book does an Indian grandfather make a treaty to bring food to a character if, in return, he will teach his grandson how to read?

4. In which book does one character show another how to make fish hooks and a snare to catch small game?

5. In which book does the story of Robinson Crusoe bring a two boys from different cultures closer to an understanding?

Sign of the Dove

Susan Fletcher. Atheneum, 1996. ISBN 0-689-80460-1 (hc); ISBN 0-689-82449-1 (pb).
URL: www.amazon.com/exec/obidos/ASIN/0689804601/qid=968190007/sr=1-1/002-9236433-5574402
Subjects: fantasy

Questions

1. In which book must green-eyed children be hidden from the queen's soldiers?

2. In which book is it believed that the heart of a dragon protects against weapons of iron?

3. In which book are young orphans abandoned when a mother dragon is killed?

4. In which book is a character able to reach into the minds of birds?

5. In which book does a boatload of children escape pursuers by shouting and banging on iron pots and pans?

Sixth Grade Can Really Kill You

Barthe De Clements. Puffin, 1995. ISBN 0-14-037130-3.
Subjects: school stories

Questions

1. In which book does a mother disagree with her daughter's wish for help in reading?

2. In which book does a character oppose being sent to special education because

she's afraid her friends will tease her?

3. In which book does Helen play practical jokes in school?

4. In which book does a character shoot off firecrackers in school and in camp?

5. In which book does someone feel she's dumb because of her reading problems, even though she is smart in other things?

Skellig

David Almond. Delacorte, 1998. ISBN 0-385-32653-X.
URL: www.falcon.jmu.edu/~ramseyil/almond.htm
     www.achuka.co.uk/daint.htm
Subjects: contemporary issues; families; fantasy

Questions

1. In which book does a character encounter a mysterious stranger in the tumble-down garage of his new home?

2. In which book is a character's baby sister very sick?

3. In which book is a character told that shoulder blades are where people's wings once grew?

4. In which book does a character study at home because she and her mother believe that school inhibits the intelligence of children?

5. In which book is a strange creature fed Chinese take-out food in an attic?

Slam

Walter Dean Myers. Scholastic, 1996. ISBN 0-590-48668-3.
URL: www.scils.rutgers.edu/special/kay/myers.html
     teacher.scholastic.com/authorsandbooks/authors/myers/bio.htm
Awards: Coretta Scott King
Subjects: school stories

Questions

1. In which book is a boy's grandmother dying?

2. In which book has a character transferred from one high school to a magnet high school for the visual arts.

3. In which book is someone jealous because the other basketball star is getting all the offers?

4. In which book does a character find out his best friend is dealing drugs?

5. In which book does someone lose the video camera his brother has borrowed from the school?

The Slave Dancer

Paula Fox. Bantam Doubleday Dell, 1997. ISBN 0-440-96132-7.
URL: www.randomhouse.com/teachers/authors/pfox.html

www.indiana.edu/~eric_rec/ieo/bibs/fox.html
Awards: Newbery
Study Guides: LL; Novel Units, Portals; LIFT
Subjects: historical fiction

Questions

1. In which book do two characters escape a ship carrying illegal cargo?

2. In which book are the black people dropped into the sea when an American ship comes too close?

3. In which book is a character imprisoned on a ship because he can play a fife?

4. In which book does a ship's cargo consist of 98 men, women, and children?

5. In which book was the first mate dropped overboard because he killed a black man who was worth good money?

Smoky, the Cow Horse

Will James. Buccaneer, 1997. ISBN 1-56849-236-7.
URL: www.willjames.com/
Awards: Newbery
Subjects: animal stories

Questions

1. Which book tells the story of a wild horse and a cowboy?

2. In which book does someone find a former bucking horse mistreated and hitched to a vegetable wagon?

3. Which book is supposed to be a true story about a cow pony?

4. In which book does a pony become a killer bronc?

5. In which book is a bucking horse known as "The Cougar"?

Snowdrops for Cousin Ruth

Susan Katz. Simon & Schuster, 1998. ISBN 0-689-813910 (hc).
URL: www.netaxs.com/~katz/
Subjects: contemporary issues; grief and death

Questions

1. In which book has a child not spoken for a whole year?

2. In which book does the school bully fall into a pond while being initiated into the Sillygross Club?

3. In which book does a character talk with her little brother after he is killed by a car skidding on ice?

4. In which book does an elderly woman make a carousel from an old phonograph turntable?

5. In which book does a family dance to the Skater's Waltz at a special birthday party?

SOS Titanic

Eve Bunting. Harcourt, 1996. ISBN 0-15-200271-5
URL: www.friend.ly.net/scoop/biographies/buntingeve/index.html
Subjects: historical fiction

Questions

1. In which book does a character find himself on the same ship with his sworn enemies?

2. In which book is someone's companion/guardian also guarding a suitcase full of jewels?

3. In which book does the cabin steward tell a character he can see disaster coming?

4. In which book does a character have to face up to his fears to get his grandpop's glove back?

5. In which book does a character rescue a girl from the icy Atlantic?

Sounder

William Armstrong. HarperCollins, 1969. ISBN 0-06-020143-6.
URL: www.edupaperback.org/authorbios/armstro.html
Awards: Newbery
Study Guides: LL; Portals; Lit. U.; Novel Units; LIFT; RBB
Subjects: animals; historical fiction

Questions

1. In which book does a mother sell walnuts to feed her family?

2. In which book does a hound dog die soon after his master does?

3. In which book does a character practice reading with old newspapers?

4. In which book does someone get prison time for stealing a ham?

5 . In which book does someone follow chain gangs across the South while looking for his father?

Sparrows in the Scullery

Barbara Brooks Wallace. Atheneum, 1997. ISBN 0-68981585-9.
Subjects: historical fiction; mystery

Questions

1. In which book is a rich little orphan kidnapped and taken to the Broggin Home for Boys?

2. In which book is someone in a workhouse given an new name?

3. In which book do some orphan boys make a clubhouse in a tunnel?

4. In which book does a kidnapped boy's reading skills lead to his rescue?

5. In which book does a character's uncle own a glass factory where children are worked to death?

Stealing Freedom

Elisa Carbone. Knopf, 1998. ISBN 0-679-99307-X.
URL: www2.lhric.org/pocantico/tubman/links.htm
Subjects: historical fiction—Underground Railroad; strong female

Questions

1. In which book is a father saving his small earnings to buy freedom for his wife and children?

2. In which book do black slaves disguise their church services as picnics?

3. In which book does a character try to find out her own birthday date?

4. In which book does a slave girl trick a white child into teaching her to read?

5. In which book does a character rescue her benefactor from vicious dogs by feeding them bread and bacon?

Stone Fox

John Gardiner. Houghton Mifflin, 1995. ISBN 0-395-73247-6.
URL: www.edupaperback.org/authorbios/gardiner.html
Study Guides: Portals; Lit. U.; Novel Units; LEAP
Subjects: animals

Questions

1. In which book did the man from the state of Wyoming tell a character he must pay $500.00, or his farm would be taken away?

2. In which book does a dog die only 10 feet from the finish line?

3. In which book did a character enter the dog sled races because he needed money to save his farm?

4. In which book does an Indian walk to the finish line so someone else could win a race?

5. In which book does someone use his winnings to buy back the Shoshone lands?

Stotan

Chris Crutcher. Bantam Doubleday Dell, 1988. ISBN 0-440-20080-6.
URL: www.scils.rutgers.edu/special/kay/crutcher.html
Subjects: contemporary issues; prejudice; sports

Questions

1. Which book title means a cross between a Stoic and a Spartan?

2. In which book does the bond forged among the members of a sports team help them cope with major problems?

3. In which book does a character plan to get even with some bullies by pushing their truck into a creek?

4. In which book do a coach and a principal tell a bully to report his problem to someone who cares?

5. In which book do two characters date, even though both their fathers are against interracial friendships?

A String in the Harp

Nancy Bond. Simon & Schuster, 1976. ISBN 0-689-80445-8 (pb).
URL: www.missy.shef.ac.uk/~emp94ms/wales.html
Subjects: fantasy

Questions

1. In which book does a family go to live in a small town in Wales?

2. In which book does a character watch scenes from ancient times after finding a very old key?

3. In which book do people have names like "Hugh-the-Bus" or "Will-the-Shop"?

4. In which book does the chicken catch fire when a character cooks her very first dinner?

5. In which book is an honored bard carried to his hidden tomb?

Stuart Little

E. B. White. HarperCollins, 1945. ISBN # 0-06-026396-7. Musical version by E.B. White and Joseph Robinette. Dramatic Publications, 1993. ISBN # 00-87129-239-4.
URL: www.umcs.maine.edu/~orono/projects/samm/facts.html
Awards: Newbery
Subjects: animals

Questions

1. In which book does the new baby in the family seem to resemble an animal?

2. In which book does an animal sail a schooner in a race across a pond in Central Park?

3. In which book does the main character get dumped on a garbage scow that is being towed out to sea?

4. In which book does an animal substitute for a teacher at Public School #7 who has fallen ill?

5. In which book does someone travel in a miniature car that can become invisible as he searches for a lost bird?

The Subtle Knife

Phillip Pullman. Knopf, 1997. ISBN 0-679-87925-0 (hc).
URL: www.puffin.co.uk/living/aut_41.html
    http://teacher.scholastic.com/authorsandbooks/authors/pullman/bio.htm
Subjects: fantasy

Questions

1. In which book does a stray cat lead a character through a hidden window in the air and into a different world?

2. In which book are peoples of the Arctic regions confused by mysterious changes in the atmosphere?

3. In which book does an aeronaut repair his damaged balloon after witches guide him to their homeland?

4. In which book has a bridge been created, joining together several different worlds?

5. In which book does a character find his father, an explorer who has been missing for many years?

Summer of the Monkeys

Wilson Rawls. Bantam, 1992. ISBN 0-553-29818-6.
URL: www.edupaperback.org/authorbios/rawlswi.html
Study Guides: LL; Novel Units; LIFT
Subjects: animals

Questions

1. In which book do a character and his hound dog discover some circus animals in the trees near his home?

2. In which book does a character's sister need an operation for a twisted leg?

3. In which book does a character set out to earn the reward money for some animals that have escaped from a circus train?

4. In which book do some animals become tipsy and ill from drinking the contents of a still?

5. In which book does a character use the reward money to pay for his sister's badly needed operation instead of buying the horse he wanted?

The Summer of the Swans

Betsy Byars. Viking, 1985. ISBN 0-670-68190.
URL: www.betsybyars.com/
Awards: Newbery
Study Guides: LL; Portals; Lit. U.; Novel Units; LIFT; RBB
Subjects: contemporary issues; handicaps

Questions

1. In which book does a character discover that a boy is not a thief after all?

2. In which book does a character spend hours looking for her lost brother?

3. In which book is a child with disabilities fascinated by watching the large white birds on a lake?

4. In which book does a character feel that she's not pretty, not a good dancer, not anything?

5. In which book does a character decide to look for some birds during the night?

Tangerine

Edward Bloor. Harcourt Brace, 1997. ISBN 0-15-201246-X (hc); ISBN 0-590-43277-X (pb).
URL: www.westga.edu/~kidreach/tangerinebkrvw.html
Subjects: contemporary issues; school stories

Questions

1. In which book is a star soccer goalie legally blind?

2. In which book does a sink hole swallow up half a middle school?

3. In which book does a character make new friends and lose an older one by working on a class project?

4. In which book is a football star struck by lightning during practice?

5. In which book are a character's suspicions of his older brother proven to be true?

Tarot Says Beware

Betsy Byars. Viking Penguin, 1995. ISBN 0-670-85575-8.
URL: www.betsybyars.com/
Subjects: mystery

Questions

1. In which book does a parrot's escape indicate trouble for his master?

2. In which book is a character alone in the house with a murderer?

3. In which book is a friend nicknamed "Meat"?

4. In which book does a puppeteer frighten a woman by making a puppet look just like her?

5. In which book does a woman have a premonition that she will be killed with a knife?

There's a Boy in the Girls' Bathroom

Louis Sachar. Knopf, 1987. ISBN 0-394-80572-0.
URL: www.falcon.jmu.edu/~ramseyil/sachar.htm
Study Guides: Portals; Novel Units; LEAP
Subjects: humor; school stories

Questions

1. In which book is a character described as looking like a good spitter?

2. In which book is a character confused when someone actually wants to be his friend?

3. In which book does the school counselor keep saying that all she can do is to help kids think for themselves?

4. In which book do two boys blame each other for their black eyes, rather than letting others know that they came from a girl?

5. In which book does a fifth grader get invited to his very first birthday party?

There's an Owl in the Shower

Jean Craighead George. HarperCollins, 1995. ISBN 0-06-440-6822.
URL: www.falcon.jmu.edu/~ramseyil/george.htm
Subjects: contemporary issues

Questions

1. In which book do you learn about hunger streaks in feathers?

2. In which book do we learn of the effect of muddy water on the life of a salmon?

3. In which book is the result of clear cutting told from two points of view?

4. In which book does someone lose his job because of an endangered animal?

5. In which book are a father and a teacher arrested because they were fighting?

The Thief

Megan Whalen Turner. Puffin, 1997. ISBN 0-688-14627-9.
URL: www.indiana.edu/~eric_rec/ieo/bibs/turner.html
Awards: Newbery
Subjects: adventure

Questions

1. In which book is someone in prison because of his boastfulness?

2. In which book is a character taken on a special quest to steal a sacred object?

3. In which book does an ancient stone determine the rightful heir to the throne?

4. In which book do a character and a scholar exchange stories of the old-time gods?

5. In which book does a character risk drowning in a cave to recover a treasure?

Through a Brief Darkness

Richard Peck. Penguin/Puffin, 1997. ISBN 0-14-038557-6.
URL: www.carr.lib.md.us/mae/peck.htm
Subjects: mystery

Questions

1. In which book does a father try to protect his daughter by keeping her away from home, in boarding schools and summer camps?

2. In which book does a character get excused from school and take an unexpected flight to London?

3. In which book does a character trust only a person she met when she was nine?

4. In which book are the aunt and uncle actually impostors?

5. In which book will you find a grandmother and two teenagers trying to foil kidnappers?

Time for Andrew: A Ghost Story

Mary Downing Hahn. Avon, 1995. ISBN 0-380-724693.
URL: www.childrensbookguild.org/hahn.html
Subjects: historical fiction

Questions

1. In which book does an aunt live in a house that looks like an Edgar Allan Poe setting?

2. In which book does a character remind his great grandfather of someone else?

3. In which book does an attic become a meeting place for kids of different generations?

4. In which book do marbles play a significant role in the story?

5. In which book are the dogs aware of changes that people don't see?

Treasure Island

Robert Louis Stevenson. Puffin, 1999. ISBN 0-14-130545-2.
URL: www.efr.hw.ac.uk/EDC/edinburghers/robert-louis-stevenson.html
         www.dreamcatchers.net/treasure/
Study Guides: LL; on-line teacher guide unit @ http://dreamcatchers.net/treasure
Subjects: adventure; classic

Questions

1. In which book do a boy, a doctor and a squire go hunting for riches?

2. In which book does someone look forward to leaving an inn and becoming a cabin boy?

3. In which book does the ship's cook turn out to be a pirate and a mutineer?

4. In which book does a character overhear a plot about killing some men and the captain?

5. In which book does someone knock out an honest sailor with his crutch before stabbing him to death?

Treasures in the Dust

Tracey Porter. HarperCollins, 1997. ISBN 0-06-027564-2 (hc); ISBN 0-06-027563-4 (pb).
URL: www.harperchildrens.com/hch/authorPage/Index.asp?authorId=12608
         www.wickespro.com/sale/0060275634
Subjects: historical fiction—Great Depression; twentieth century

Questions

1. In which book does a character play secretly with her dolls, even though she thinks she is too old?

2. In which book do two girls gather roots and leaves to help feed the family's only cow?

3. In which book are best friends parted when one family leaves their farm during a drought?

4. In which book does a character help set up a museum display after finding a rare Comanche arrow?

5. In which book does a character plant corn seeds where her family camps so she can imagine a road that will lead her home?

The Trouble with Tuck

Theodore Taylor. Doubleday, 1989. ISBN 0-385-17774-7.
URL: www.edupaperback.org/authorbios/Taylor_Theodore.html
Study Guides: LL
Subjects: animals

Questions

1. In which book does a character fall in love with a squirming, fat, yellow ball of fur?

2. In which book does a golden Labrador twice save a character's life?

3. In which book does a dog suddenly begin to go blind?

4. In which book is someone determined to find a solution to an animal's sudden blindness?

5. In which book does a character devote herself to keeping an animal's blindness from ending his life?

The True Confessions of Charlotte Doyle

Avi. Orchard, 1990. ISBN 0-531-05893-X.
URL: www.avi-writer.com
  www.carr.org/read/fiction.html
Awards: Newbery
Study Guides: LL; Portals; Novel Units; LIFT; RBB
Subjects: historical fiction

Questions

1. In which book does someone learn to climb the rigging, throw a knife, swab the deck, and scrape a hull?

2. In which book is a character given a knife used in a murder?

3. In which book does a Black man tell a character they have two things in common?

4. In which book does a character discover that her loyalty should not be given to the crew but to the captain?

5. In which book does a crew sign on to a sailing ship in order to get revenge?

The Trumpet of the Swan

E.B. White. HarperCollins, 1973. ISBN 0-0644-0048-4.
URL: www.falcon.jmu.edu/~ramseyil/white.htm
  www.winsor.edu/library2/ebbiog.htm
Awards: Newbery
Study Guides: Portals; Novel Units; RBB
Subjects: animals

Questions

1. In which book does someone realize one of the cygnets doesn't speak?

2. In which book does a character decide to find Sam, so he can go to school with him?

3. In which book does a swan rescue a camper?

4. In which book does an animal get a job as a bugler?

5. In which book does an animal earn over $4000?

Tuck Everlasting

Natalie Babbitt. Farrar, Straus and Giroux, 1975. ISBN 0-374-48009-5.
URL: www.ipl.org/youth/AskAuthor/babbitt.html
Study Guides: LL; Portals; Lit. U.; Novel Units; LEAP; LIFT; RBB
Subjects: classic; fantasy

Questions

1. In which book does a character have to make a decision about whether or not to drink some water?

2. In which book is there a family that has lived forever?

3. In which book does someone help with a jail break to rescue her friend Mae?

4. In which book does a family move from place to place so that no one will notice that they never age?

5. In which book does a character pour magic water over her toad?

Twisted Summer

Willo Davis Roberts. Atheneum, 1996. ISBN 0-689-80459-8
URL: www.cbcbooks.org/navigation/autindex.htm
Subjects: mystery

Questions

1. In which book does someone hope a boy will realize she is now 14 and one of the "big kids"?

2. In which book has an innocent boy been sent to prison for murder?

3. In which book does a character try to find out her step-grandfather's secret?

4. In which book is a wallet planted underneath a couch where the police will find it?

5. In which book has everything seemed to change on Crystal Lake?

Under the Blood-Red Sun

Graham Salisbury. Bantam Doubleday Dell, 1994. ISBN 0-440-41139-4.
URL: http://grahamsalisbury.com
Subjects: historical fiction—World War II; prejudice

Questions

1. In which book does a grandfather get his family in trouble by keeping the things he brought with him from the old country?

2. In which book does being both Japanese and American call for much patience to avoid bringing shame on the family?

3. In which book are some birds killed by soldiers?

4. In which book are fishing boats sunk to prevent them from helping the enemy, unless they fly an American flag?

5. In which book do we learn that the most valuable thing we have is our freedom to make choices—the power over our own lives?

Up a Road Slowly

Irene Hunt. Silver Burdett, 1993. ISBN 0-382-24366-8.
URL: www.edupaperback.org/authorbios/Hunt_Irene
Awards: Newbery
Study Guides: LL
Subjects: school stories

Questions

1. In which book do the some characters declare someone they dislike is a queen, so they won't have to sit with her at lunch?

2. In which book is someone unhappy when she's sent to live with her aunt after her mother dies?

3. In which book does Cordelia give up teaching when the country school is closed?

4. In which book does a character choose to live with her aunt, even though it means she has little social life?

5. In which book does someone discover that a handsome character dates her only to get her to do his schoolwork?

The View from Saturday

E.L. Konigsburg. Aladdin, 1998. ISBN 0-689-81721-5.
URL: http://teacher.scholastic.com/authorsandbooks/authors/konigs/bio.htm
Awards: Newbery
Study Guides: LL; Portals; Lit. U.; Novel Units; Scholastic
Subjects: contemporary issues

Questions

1. In which book does a character's summer visit to his grandparents have surprising links to school in the fall?

2. In which book do we learn about sea turtles and the volunteers that work to help them survive?

3. In which book will we find that a tea once a week cements a friendship among four kids?

4. In which book do the answers to contest questions draw on personal experiences of the contestants?

5. In which book does the new kid in school find that secret messages are a way to attract those kids he wants as friends?

The Volcano Disaster

Peg Kehret. Pocket Books, 1998. ISBN 0-671-00969-9.
URL: www.eduplace.com/kids/hmr/mtai/Kehret.html
Subjects: fantasy

Questions

1. In which book does a character move into a bedroom filled with his inventor grandfather's project plans?

2. In which book does a 27-page diary format school report get an A+?

3. In which book do we learn about an organization called "Purebred Dog Rescue"?

4. In which book does the Instant Commuter take a character and girl on a trip through space and time?

5. In which book does a character get hit with hot mud balls?

Wait till Helen Comes: A Ghost Story

Mary Downing Hahn. Avon, 1986. ISBN 0-3807-0442-0.
URL: www.childrensbookguild.org/hahn.html
Subjects: mystery

Questions

1. In which book do two characters investigate the legend of the haunted Harper house?

2. In which book are two characters trapped in the cellar of a haunted house?

3. In which book does Heather, the character's sister, become involved with a child ghost?

4. In which book is there a graveyard with a mysterious, overgrown tombstone bearing the initials of a little girl?

5. In which book is someone afraid that her father won't love her if he learns her secret about a long ago fire?

A Walk in Wolf Wood

Mary Stewart. Fawcett, 1982. ISBN 0-449-21422-2.
URL: www.ub.rug.nl/camelot/intervws/stewart.html
Subjects: fantasy

Questions

1. In which book do some children follow a weeping man?

2. In which book do some children find themselves back in medieval Germany?

3. In which book does a gold amulet help prove that a wolf is really a duke's trusted friend?

4. In which book does someone pretend to be the page who makes the duke's bedtime drink?

5. In which book does an enchanter take a character hostage after he finds her in his secret room?

Walk Two Moons

Sharon Creech. HarperCollins, 1994. ISBN 0-06-023337-0.
URL: http://falcon.jmu.edu/~ramseyil/creech.htm
Awards: Newbery
Study Guides: LL; Portals; Novel Units; LIFT; RBB
Subjects: families; journeys

Questions

1. In which book does a character relate the wild tales told by her friend?

2. Which book is about Salamanca Tree Hiddle?

3. In which book is a grandmother bitten by a water moccasin?

4. In which book does a fourteen-year-old drive the car through Idaho by herself?

5. In which book does a character flinch every time a boy puts his hand on her arm?

Wanted!

Caroline B. Cooney. Scholastic, 1997. ISBN 0-590-98849-2.
URL: http://teacher.scholastic.com/authorsandbooks/authors/cooney/bio.htm
Subjects: mystery

Questions

1. In which book is a computer disk, labeled "TWIN," a key to a murderer?

2. In which book does a character follow her father's orders to drive his beloved Corvette, when she doesn't even have her license?

3. In which book does an email message seem to convince a character of someone's guilt?

4. In which book does a high schooler hide out in a college dorm?

5. In which book does a high school class leave school to hunt for a missing classmate?

The Warm Place

Nancy Farmer. Penguin, 1995. ISBN 0-14-037956-8.
URL: www.edupaperback.org/authorbios/farmerna.html
Subjects: humor

Questions

1. In which book do we meet "slopes" or demons who were directed to spread misery throughout the world?

2. In which book do we meet a character who can talk with a rat, a chameleon, and a giraffe?

3. In which book do Sargasso Strangleweeds grow from the size of hairs to becoming as thick as fire hoses?

4. In which book is home defined as a warm place in your mind?

5. In which book are humans called hairless monkeys and the sneakiest creatures alive?

The Watcher

James Howe. Atheneum, 1997. ISBN 0-689-80186-6.
URL: www.fcps.k12.va.us/FairviewES/reading/howe.htm
Subjects: families

Questions

1. In which book does someone imagine she is part of an ideal family?

2. In which book does a character view a lifeguard as a guardian angel?

3. In which book does someone feel he is a loser—just like Holden Caulfield?

4. In which book is a lifeguard afraid that he won't be able to save people from drowning?

5. In which book does someone summon the police by playing sad music as loud as possible?

Watership Down

Richard Adams. Macmillan, 1974. ISBN 0-02-700030-3.
URL: www.watershipdown.org
Study Guides: LL
Subjects: animals

Questions

1. In which book do some animals take care of a wounded gull?

2. In which book do the main characters speak the Lapine Language?

3. In which book is there a final battle between General Woundwort and Bigwig?

4. In which book are some of the characters named Fiver and Blackberry?

5. In which book do some animals search for a new warren?

The Watsons Go to Birmingham—1963

Christopher Paul Curtis. Delacorte, 1995. ISBN 0-385-32175-9.
URL: www.falcon.jmu.edu/~ramseyil/curtis.htm
     http://teacher.scholastic.com/authorsandbooks/authors/curtis/bio.htm
Awards: Newbery
Study Guides: LL; LIFT
Subjects: contemporary issues; families; prejudice

Questions

1. In which book does someone's brother get his lips frozen to the mirror on a car?

2. In which book does someone shave off all his son's hair?

3. In which book is a character rescued from a whirlpool, which he calls the "Wool Pooh"?

4. In which book is a character so upset that he crawls behind the couch, where the "World Famous Pet Hospital" is located?

5. In which book is a character upset with himself because he was too scared to rescue anyone from a church bombing?

Weasel

Cynthia DeFelice. Macmillan, 1990. ISBN 0-02-72647-2.
URL: www.maquoketa.k12.ia.us/defelice.html
    www.carolhurst.com/titles/weasel.html
Study Guides: LL; Novel Units
Subjects: historical fiction

Questions

1. Which book tells about the different paths taken by two Indian fighters? One adopts the ways of the Indian, while the other takes up killing.

2. In which book does someone brood all winter about not killing his captor?

3. In which book is a stone wall used for messages and gifts of medicine, moccasins, and seed corn?

4. In which book do two children follow a strange silent man who has their mother's gold locket?

5. In which book does someone save a man from losing his leg after he's been caught in an animal trap?

The Westing Game

Ellen Raskin. Viking Penguin, 1997. ISBN 0-14038664-5.
URL: www.edupaperback.org/authorbios/raskin_Ellen.html
Awards: Newbery
Study Guides: LL; Portals; Novel Units; LIFT; RBB
Subjects: mystery

Questions

1. In which book does someone solve a mystery but keep the solution to herself?

2. In which book are 16 heirs to a millionaire's fortune given some strange sets of clues?

3. In which book are six families mysteriously invited to buy six luxury apartments?

4. In which book are parts of a patriotic song used as clues to a mystery?

5. In which book does a millionaire pretend to be one of his own heirs?

What Happened in Hamelin

Gloria Skurzynski. Peter Smith, 1995. ISBN 0-8446-6268-1.
URL: www.gloriabooks.com/
Subjects: historical fiction

Questions

1. In which book is a character called a name meaning "Ghost," because he's usually covered with white flour?

2. In which book does Geist get together with a stranger named Gast?

3. In which book do some town animals carry the plague?

4. In which book does the stranger want rye-infested ergot put into the sweetmeat buns?

5. In which book are children taken from a town to be sold to a far-away nobleman?

Where the Red Fern Grows

Wilson Rawls. Bantam, 1974. ISBN 0-055-327-4295.
URL: www.randomhouse.com/teachers/guides/wher.html
Study Guides: LL; Portals; Lit. U.; Novel Units; LIFT; RBB; Sch.
Subjects: animals; classic

Questions

1. In which book does a character train his dogs to win a coon hunt contest?

2. In which book did Little Ann and Old Dan win a championship coon hunt?

3. Which book is about a character who receives a gold cup for winning a contest with some animals?

4. In which book are some animals killed by a mountain lion?

5. In which book does a character earn money to buy two hounds?

The Whipping Boy

Sid Fleischman. Troll, 1986. ISBN 0-816-71038-4.
URL: http://teacher.scholastic.com/authorsandbooks/authors/fleischman/bio.htm
     www.carr.lib.md.us/authco/fleischman/htm
Awards: Newbery
Study Guides: Portals; Lit. U.; Novel Units; LEAP
Subjects: adventure

Questions

1. In which book is it forbidden for anyone to spank, thrash, or whack a prince?

2. In which book do two runaway characters end up being kidnapped by two outlaws?

3. In which book are two characters rescued from a thrashing by someone who sics her bear on the outlaws?

4. In which book do two boys make friends with a character and a dancing bear?

5. In which book do some characters with strange names kidnap two boys for a royal ransom?

Whirligig

Paul Fleischman. Holt, 1998. ISBN 0-8050-5582-7.
URL: www.eduplace.com/kids/hmr/mtai/fleischman.html
     www.indiana.edu/~eric_rec/ieo/bibs/fleisp.html
Subjects: contemporary issues; journeys

Questions

1. In which book is someone totally concerned with acting like the cool kids in his new school?

2. In which book does a sixteen-year-old kill someone while driving while drunk?

3. In which book is a character asked to set up four memorials to a victim—one in each corner of the United States?

4. In which book do we see how some characters' lives are changed by some strange wooden artwork?

5. In which book does a long bus journey of atonement make someone realize his own life is interlocked with others?

The White Dragon

Anne McCaffrey. Ballantine, 1979. ISBN 0-345-27567-5 (hc); ISBN 0-34534-1678 (pb).
URL: www.annemccaffrey.org/
Subjects: fantasy

Questions

1. In which book does a character learn to fly a dragon runt?

2. In which book does a character teach an animal to chew firestone?

3. In which book does a character find evidence of the Old Ones at a plateau?

4. In which book does a character ride a runner named Stupid?

5. In which book does a character become a Lord Holder?

Who Killed Mr. Chippendale? A Mystery in Poems

Mel Glenn. Dutton Lodestar Books, 1996. ISBN 0-525-67530-2.
URL: www.yabooks.about.com/teens/yabooks/library/authors/bl_melglenn.htm
Subjects: contemporary issues; mystery; school stories

Questions

1. In which book is the entire story told in verse?

2. In which book do we learn bits of the story from the viewpoints of the high school students involved?

3. In which book does the guidance counselor find the answers to a story?

4. In which book do we see examples of the impact a teacher can have on his students—both good and bad?

5. Which book is about an incredibly diverse group of students?

Wild Magic

Tamora Pierce. Atheneum, 1992. ISBN 0-689-31761-1 (hc); ISBN 0-679-88288-X (pb).
URL: www.dy8.co.uk/tamora/
      www.sff.net/people/Tamora.Pierce/bio2.html
Subjects: fantasy; strong female

Questions

1. In which book is someone hired to drive a herd of ponies south to the capital city?

2. In which book does a character wear a badger's claw as a talisman?

3. In which book are girls allowed to serve as soldiers in the Queen's Riders?

4. In which book are a castle's defenders attacked by foul-smelling creatures?

5. In which book does a pod of whales refuse a request to join battle against invaders?

Williwaw

Tom Bodett. Knopf, 1999. ISBN 0-679-99030-5 (hc)
URL: www.tombodett.com/
Subjects: Alaska; contemporary issues; survival

Questions

1. In which book are some characters left alone in a wilderness cabin while their father is out fishing?

2. In which book does playing a computer game cause serious trouble for a character and his sister?

3. In which book do two children find their way in a fog by following the smell of French fries?

4. In which book are some people caught in a storm when they stay too long at a party?

5. In which book does a grouchy neighbor help rescue two survivors of a storm?

Willow King

Chris Platt. Random House, 1998. ISBN 0-679-98655-3 (hc).
URL: www.equineonly.com/randomhouse/willowking.htm
Subjects: animals; contemporary issues

Questions

1. In which book does a character trade her most cherished possession to save the life of a newborn animal?

2. In which book does a character throw a pine cone at someone she really likes?

3. In which book do some characters restore a neglected Appaloosa to his original elegant appearance?

4. In which book do horses recover from leg injuries by swimming in a pool?

5. In which book does a two-year-old win an important race?

The Winter Room

Gary Paulson. Bantam Doubleday Dell, 1998. ISBN 0-440-22783-6.
URL: www.ipl.org/youth/AskAuthor/paulsen.html
www.randomhouse.com/features/garypaulsen
Awards: Newbery
Subjects: families

Questions

1. In which book does an uncle keep telling tales of the old country, until one of his nephews says he's a liar?

2. Which book tells of the joys and the hard times of living on a Minnesota farm?

3. In which book does old Uncle David pick up an axe in each hand, raise them both high over his head, and swing them into two ends of a log?

4. In which book did someone try to jump from the barn onto the back of a draft horse, just as the hero did in one of the Zane Grey books he was reading?

5. In which book does Crazy Alen continue to play jokes on the foreman, not only after he's fired, but even after he's dead?

The Witch of Blackbird Pond

Elizabeth Speare. Dell, 1958. ISBN 0-440-99577-9.
URL: www.randomhouse.com/teachers/guides/witc.html
Awards: Newbery
Study Guides: LL; Portals; Lit. U.; Novel Units; LEAP; LIFT
Subjects: historical fiction

Questions

1. Which book tells about Quaker Hannah, among others?

2. In which book are jack-o-lanterns considered sinful?

3. In which book is an old woman who lives by herself blamed for the plague?

4. In which book is a character thought to be a witch because she knows how to swim?

5. In which book is someone accused of witchcraft because she taught a child to read the Bible?

The Wolves of Willoughby Chase

Joan Aiken. Dell, 1987. ISBN 0-440-49603-9.
URL: http://falcon.jmu.edu/~ramseyil/aiken.htm
Subjects: mystery

Questions

1. In which book is a diet of bread and water given to children who displease their governess?

2. In which book does tattling on someone earn you a piece of cheese?

3. In which book do geese help catch a criminal?

4. In which book does a pack of animals stop a train?

5. In which book does a white curtain become a poor girl's clothes?

Words of Stone

Kevin Henkes. Greenwillow, 1992. ISBN 0-688-11356-7 (hc).
URL: http://falcon.jmu.edu/~ramseyil/henkes.htm
Subjects: contemporary issues

Questions

1. In which book does a character try to overcome his fear of riding a Ferris wheel?

2. In which book is a character left with her grandmother because her mother wants a vacation?

3. In which book does a character bury his imaginary friend every year?

4. In which book does a character collect old keys to open the locked doors he finds in his dreams?

5. In which book does a character steal a small animal from a someone's Noah's ark set?

The Wreckers

Iain Lawrence. Delacorte, 1998. ISBN 0-385-32535-5 (hc); ISBN 0-440-41545-4 (pb).
URL: www.bcbooks.com/ilawrence.html
Subjects: historical fiction; sea stories

Questions

1. In which book does a ship called the "Isle of Skye" go down off the coast of Cornwall?

2. In which book does a huge man on a black horse rescue a character from a mob determined to kill him?

3. In which book does a character find his missing father by whistling a tune from his childhood?

4. In which book does a man freed from chains shoot his rescuer and throw him over a cliff?

5. In which book is a cargo of second-rate wine believed to be a shipment of gold?

The Wright Brothers: How They Invented the Airplane

Russell Freedman. Holiday, 1991. ISBN 0-8234-0875-2.
URL: www.indiana.edu/~eric_rec/ieo/bibs/freedman.html
Awards: Newbery
Subjects: biography

Questions

1. In which book do men trained for water life-saving make up an aircraft ground crew?

2. In which book do two inventors own a printing press, a bicycle shop, and a dark room for photographic prints?

3. In which book do some characters want a list of the country's windiest places?

4. Which biography has illustrations made in the beginning of the 1900s by its subjects?

5. In which book does a mechanically minded parent make a sled for her children?

Wringer

Jerry Spinelli. HarperCollins, 1997. ISBN 0-06-024913-7.
URL: www.carr.lib.md.us/authco/spinelli-j.htm
    http://teacher.scholastic.com/authorsandbooks/authors/spinelli/bio.htm
Awards: Newbery

Study Guides: LIFT
Subjects: school stories

Questions

1. In which book does a character go along with his gang when they decide to pick on his friend Dorothy?

2. In which book do boys celebrate their ninth birthdays by getting knuckled by Farquar?

3. In which book is a character adopted by a pigeon?

4. In which book does a town raise money for their parks by shooting animals?

5. In which book do some characters invent a game called "tree stumping"?

A Wrinkle in Time

Madeleine L'Engle. Dell, 1976. ISBN : 0-440-99805-0.
URL: wwwvms.utexas.edu/~eithlan/lengle.html (Note: accessible via the University of Texas site.)
http://teacher.scholastic.com/authorsandbooks/authors/lengle/bio.htm
Awards: Newbery
Study Guides: LL; Portals; Lit. U.; Novel Units; LEAP; RBB; Sch.
Subjects: fantasy

Questions

1. In which book does a disembodied, oversized brain give commands from a strange domed building?

2. In which book do some characters meet Mrs Who, Mrs Which, and Mrs Whatsit?

3. In which book is someone captured by an evil brain?

4. In which book does a character's love for her little brother defeat the power of IT?

5. What is a tesseract? (The answer is the title of the book.)

The Year of the Black Pony

Walt Morey. Blue Heron Pub, 1989. ISBN 0-936085-14-2.
URL: www.teleport.com/~bhp/a_authors/a_Morey.html
Subjects: animals; historical fiction

Questions

1. In which book does a woman call her husband Mr. Shaw, instead by his first name?

2. In which book does someone suggest a pebble in an animal's ear will keep it too busy to fight its rider?

3. In which book does a character almost die from riding to get a teddy bear for someone ill?

4. Which book is about a 4th of July bucking horse that "couldn't be broke"?

5. In which book does someone insist that the man who caused her husband's death will have to marry her and help support her family?

Reproducible Bookmarks and Badges

Use any or all of the following reproducible bookmark and badge patterns to promote your Battle of the Books competition. The "Fact Tracker" bookmark is also a good way to help students keep track of important information about each book while they are reading.

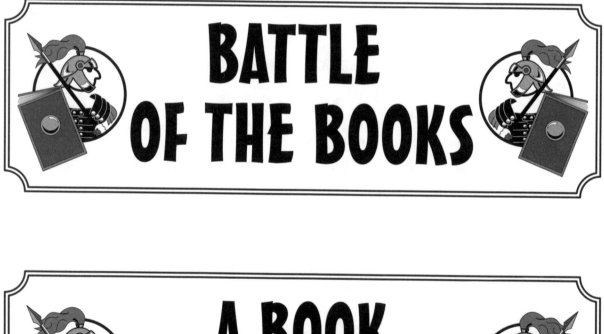

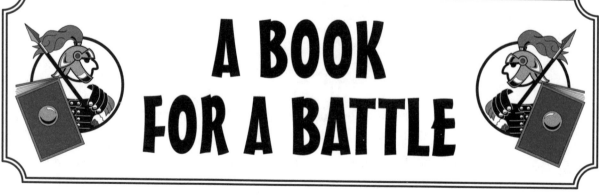

Bookmark patterns

Battle of the Books
Fact Tracker

Book Title: _____

Author: _____

Main Characters: _____

_____

Setting — Place: _____

Time: _____

Main Events or Problems: _____

_____

Summary of the Book: _____

_____

Interesting Detail: _____

Fact Tracker pattern This bookmark was recreated with permission from Purdy Elementary School, Fort Atkinson, WI.

Badge patterns

Author, Subject and Award Index

Authors

Subjects

A

Adventure

Alaska

Animals

B

Biography

C

Classic

Contemporary Issues

F

Families

Coretta Scott King Award and Honor Books

Newbery Award and Honor Books